FAN PHENOMENA

AUDREY HEPBURN

EDITED BY
JACQUI MILLER

Credits

First Published in the UK in 2014 by Intellect Books,
The Mill, Parnall Road, Fishponds, Bristol, BS16 3JG, UK

First Published in the USA in 2014 by Intellect Books,
The University of Chicago Press, 1427 E. 60th Street,
Chicago, IL 60637, USA

Editor: Jacqui Miller

Series Editor and Design: Gabriel Solomons

Typesetting: Stephanie Sarlos

Copy Editor: Emma Rhys

A Catalogue record for this book is available from
the British Library

Fan Phenomena Series
ISSN: 2051-4468
eISSN: 2051-4476

Fan Phenomena: Audrey Hepburn
ISBN: 978-1-78320-206-5
eISBN: 978-1-78320-234-8 / 978-1-78320-235-5

Printed and bound by
Bell & Bain Limited, Glasgow

<u>Contents</u>

Acknowledgements

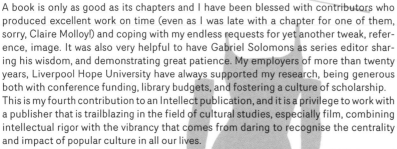

A book is only as good as its chapters and I have been blessed with contributors who produced excellent work on time (even as I was late with a chapter for one of them, sorry, Claire Molloy!) and coping with my endless requests for yet another tweak, reference, image. It was also very helpful to have Gabriel Solomons as series editor sharing his wisdom, and demonstrating great patience. My employers of more than twenty years, Liverpool Hope University have always supported my research, being generous both with conference funding, library budgets, and fostering a culture of scholarship. This is my fourth contribution to an Intellect publication, and it is a privilege to work with a publisher that is trailblazing in the field of cultural studies, especially film, combining intellectual rigor with the vibrancy that comes from daring to recognise the centrality and impact of popular culture in all our lives.

I'd particularly like to thank my daughter Jemma Jones, whose birthday card really triggered my idea for this book; we're well on the way, through granddaughter, Charlotte, to establishing a family dynasty of Audrey fans. Thanks also go to a range of friends and colleagues, some of whom contributed chapters – Lynn Hilditch, Francis Vose, Esperanza Miyake, and Claire Molloy, for offering me endless new examples of Audrey-ness.

Jacqui Miller, Editor

Introduction
Jacqui Miller

→ To her millions of fans, Audrey Hepburn remains the most revered and influential film star to have graced the silver screen. However, Audrey (her fans feel they know her and are on first-name terms) is much more than a 'mere' film star. On the one hand, she was a girl of Dutch-Irish aristocratic lineage who experienced her girlhood in war-deprived occupied Holland, grew up to become an astonishingly beautiful, talented and successful actress and Hollywood star, before devoting herself to motherhood and goodwill work for UNICEF.

'Audrey' is also a multifaceted accumulation of images – fashion plates by photographers such as Cecil Beaton showcasing designs by Hubert de Givenchy, and particularly a series of iconographic film characters including Princess Ann in *Roman Holiday* (William Wyler, 1953) Sabrina Fairchild in *Sabrina* (Billy Wilder, 1954) and especially, Holly Golightly in *Breakfast at Tiffany's* (Blake Edwards, 1961). In her own 'real' life and in her 'reel' work, Audrey Hepburn, the flesh and blood woman, is present, but 'Audrey' long since became something much more: 'Audrey' is a cultural and fan phenomenon. Just the words 'so Audrey' or 'very Audrey' have specific meaning: elegance, grace, timeless chic. Since the early death of Audrey Hepburn in 1993, 'Audrey' as a phenomenon has continued to proliferate to the extent that her own name is not always needed: the phenomenon is also encapsulated in a range of related commodity-signifiers. At the present moment (December 2012), UK weekday ITV1 breakfast television show, *Daybreak*, is featuring its annual 'Little Black Dress Diet', and in a very different sphere, paint manufacturer Crown, is marketing Little Black Dress matt emulsion. Of course these two examples do have one thing in common: they are trading on associations of 'Audrey' or Audrey-ness. The Little Black Dress Diet will persuade women that they too can have Audrey's allure, while the paint is part of the 'Fashion For Walls Indulgence' range. As Pamela Keogh has written, in words that could speak on behalf of all Audrey fans: 'since we first saw her in *Roman Holiday*, Audrey is still showing us how it's done. As a style icon, Audrey's influence is unrivalled.'

Although that influence cannot be doubted, the question is just *why*, in a world that has changed in many ways beyond all recognition, does Audrey Hepburn alone of all her movie contemporaries continue to exert this influence, not just on fashion but, as the LBD paint, reveals, all aspects of lifestyle and, as skimming through the numbers of books using her as a lifestyle guru reveals, on the way we should aspire to behave. The starting point to investigate Audrey's fan phenomena has to be her films, the body of work with which she – as opposed to the cultural proliferation of Audrey-ness – created. Their impact continues to be huge; I recently wished a friend taking a Christmas break a good 'Roman holiday', while *Breakfast at Tiffany's* plays at cinemas across the globe every February 14th. However, the films also continue to impact on cultural production: Audrey, or rather her associations with style, is frequently referenced in TV shows such as *Sex and the City* (Darren Star, HBO, 1998-2004) and *Will and Grace* (David Kohan and Max Mutchnick, NBC, 1998-2006), and the fashion magazine industry would be lost if Audrey disappeared from 'get her look' pages.

It is very difficult to imagine Audrey Hepburn surfing the net, sending a text or checking her Facebook status, although Holly Golightly might have found Google useful to check a (male) party guest's place on America's rich list, or welcomed a BlackBerry to organize her social life. However, the Internet has formed multiple opportunities for

Audrey fandom, from the posting of fanfiction, to fashion blogging, to fan-sites simply established for the sharing of information.

Fan Phenomena is as varied as both the subjects of the fandom, and the fans themselves. Because Audrey Hepburn was herself a 'real' woman, as opposed to, say, a comic book or TV show character, and because of the type of woman she was – one that epitomized good manners, good taste, self-discipline and grooming, her fan phenomena is not expressed through the campy jamborees that some fandoms manifest. Rather, Audrey fan phenomena tend to be present in print and electronic images and exchanges instead of conventions and get-togethers.

The chapters in *Fan Phenomena: Audrey Hepburn* each seek to examine aspects of Audrey-ness and so explain just what it is about her essence and legacy that continues to actually increase in fandom terms each year. In 'Audrey Hepburn: Fashion, Fairy Tales and Transformation', Lynn Hilditch examines the centrality of costume within Hepburn's films and the ways it was used as a means of making the ordinary extraordinary. This ability of Audrey's herself: the skinny girl with bushy eyebrows and crooked teeth who nonetheless was voted by New Woman Magazine the most beautiful movie star of all time in 2006, and the characters she played, such as Eliza Doolittle, the cockney flower seller who became the belle of the ball, have always been an inspiration to fans. Audrey had a 'look' women believed could be theirs. Esperanza Miyake's 'Why is Hepburn so 'Audrey?' also looks at *My Fair Lady*'s (George Cukor, 1964) Eliza Doolittle to question the nature and appeal of Audrey-ness, but instead of focusing on fashion considers the attributes of posture, voice and playfulness. That two chapters take the same film as their starting point, but 'read' Audrey-ness in different ways shows that fans will select from Audrey's image the elements that speak to them. Transformation recurs in Claire Molloy's 'Transformation, Fashion and *Funny Face*' but in this chapter, the focus is on fans' constant reconstructing of the 'Audrey' phenomenon as it is cited in new cultural forms: TV comedy-drama, advertising and music.

Similarly, two chapters, by Andrew Howe and Armen Karaoghlanian, look at the phenomenon of the 'little black dress', but again the perspectives vary. Howe studies the cultural history of the LBD. Although the LBD did not in fact originate with Hepburn, her association with the Givenchy version in *Breakfast at Tiffany's* cemented her style iconography to the point that fashion fandom can now only see the LBD filtered through the Hepburn image, glowing in the style association (as the diverse examples cited above emphasize). Karaoghlanian takes an exuberant overview of Audrey's impact on women's style from her emergence in *Roman Holiday* to the present day.

Peter Krämer's 'The Making of an International Star: The Early Film Career and Star Image of Audrey Hepburn, 1948-54' and Jacqui Miller's '"She's enchanting": How Her Neglected Films Give Fans the Key to Audrey-ness' are rooted in the intertwining of Hepburn's image, films and fandom, in other words the ways in which fans intervene, through their reading of publicity or relationship with film characters, to construct ideas of who Audrey is. Krämer looks at how publicity and its reception transforms Audrey from a naughty man-trap in her early films to a gracious international star in her first two Hollywood productions, while Miller shows that every aspect of Audrey-ness associated with the handful of 'major' films, actually has its origin or parallel in the lesser-known work. ●

GO FURTHER

Books

What Would Audrey Do? Timeless Lessons for Living with Grace and Style
Pamela Clark Keogh
(London: Aurum, 2008)

Chapter
1

Audrey Hepburn: Fashion, Fairy Tales and Transformation

Lynn Hilditch

→ Throughout the 1950s and 1960s in particular, Audrey Hepburn portrayed characters that underwent an identity transformation. In the case of Princess Ann, Sabrina Fairchild and Holly Golightly, for example, it was mostly self-motivated, but for others, such as Jo Stockton and Eliza Doolittle, it was an imposed transformation. Hepburn once admitted that she relied upon her costumes to help her construct her characters, rather like a little girl playing at dressing up.

To her, the costuming was a crucial part of the acting process, especially as she had never had any formal acting training. Audrey explained, as quoted by Melissa Hellstern in *How to be Lovely: The Audrey Hepburn Way of Life*:

Clothes, *per se*, the costume is terribly important to me, always has been. Perhaps because I didn't have any technique for acting when I started because I had never learned to act. I had a sort of make-believe, like children do.

Hepburn's ability to transform her characters so easily – tackling within the same film the opposing roles of princess/lady/socialite and girl-next-door/flower girl/chauffeur's daughter with equal conviction – is perhaps due to Hepburn having undergone her own personal off-screen identity transformation from Edda Hepburn van Heemstra, the little girl born into Dutch aristocracy in 1929 who dreamed of becoming a ballerina like her heroine Margot Fonteyn, into Audrey Hepburn, one of the most influential twentieth-century movie stars and fashion icons.

Unlike the female sex symbols of the 1950s and 1960s, such as Marilyn Monroe, Lana Turner, Jane Russell and Bridget Bardot, whose glamour and star personas appeared manufactured or contrived in order to appeal to a male audience, Hepburn was very much a 'woman's woman', appealing to a female audience through her natural beauty, individual feminine style and exceptional fashion sense. Hepburn's look of the 'modern woman' was partly due to her lifelong friendship with the French fashion designer Hubert de Givenchy whom she met on the set of *Sabrina* (Billy Wilder, 1954) in 1953 and who would design her clothes for the next forty years. Hepburn claimed, as quoted by Pamela Clarke Keogh in *Audrey Style*, that Givenchy's clothes were 'the only clothes in which I feel myself. He is far from a couturier; he is a creator of personality'. Givenchy and Hepburn collaborated on many of the costume designs for her films, creating what became known as 'The Hepburn Style', and although Edith Head won an Oscar for the Costume Design on *Sabrina* (and previously designed Hepburn's costumes for *Roman Holiday* [William Wyler, 1953]), Givenchy had provided design sketches for many of the outfits worn in the film, including Sabrina's ball gown. Therefore, it was partly due to her relationship with Givenchy, as well as the inspired use of on-screen fashion, that enabled Hepburn to create, develop and transform her characters in some of her most popular films, in particular, *Roman Holiday*, *Sabrina*, *Funny Face* (Stanley Donen, 1957), *Breakfast at Tiffany's* (Blake Edwards, 1961) and *My Fair Lady* (George Cukor, 1964).

'At midnight, I'll turn into a pumpkin and drive away in my glass slipper' (Anya, *Roman Holiday*)

Hepburn's first significant on-screen identity transformation was in William Wyler's romantic comedy *Roman Holiday* – her first Hollywood film role. In a reversal of the 'Cin-

Audrey Hepburn: Fashion, Fairy Tales and Transformation
Lynn Hilditch

*Fig. 1: Hepburn as the regal
Princess Ann in Roman
Holiday.*

derella' story, Hepburn plays the young Ruritanian Princess Ann (see Figure 1) who has become tired of her role as the personification of 'sweetness and decency' and bored of all the endless functions, conferences and parties that she is expected to go to during her demanding goodwill tour of European cities. After attending a lavish ball thrown in her honour, the princess retires to her bedchamber where she is undressed, briefed about the next day's duties and put to bed by the Countess Vereberg (Margaret Rawlings). However, her disillusionment with her restricted and rather old-fashioned royal lifestyle is apparent:

> Princess Ann: I hate this nightgown. I hate all my nightgowns, and I hate all my underwear too.
> Countess: My dear, you have lovely things.
> Princess Ann: But I'm not two hundred years old. Why can't I sleep in pyjamas?
> Countess: Pyjamas?
> Princess Ann: Just the top part. Did you know that there are people who sleep with absolutely nothing on at all?

Note how the nightgown in this scene closely resembles the nightwear that Hepburn would later wear in the 'I Could Have Danced All Night' (Frederick Loewe and Alan Jay Lerner, 1956) number in *My Fair Lady* as she begins her character transformation from the common flower girl to the lady (a reversal of her identity change in *Roman Holiday*). Hepburn's ability to combine comedy with an element of naive charm is demonstrated when the princess gets hysterical and has to be sedated by the royal doctor. Then, in an act of anesthetized rebellion, she defies the orders of the palace and escapes into the city of Rome in the back of a truck. After falling asleep on a park bench – homeless and alone in an unfamiliar city – she is rescued from her downward identity spiral by American journalist Joe Bradley (Gregory Peck), her aristocratic identity temporarily discarded and replaced by the anonymity of an ordinary (and, at first, seemingly drunk)

Fig. 2: Hepburn after her transformation into Anya/ Smitty in Roman Holiday.

tourist. In another scene, this time in Joe's apartment, the princess shows delight at escaping the constraints of her aristocratic existence – and, with it, her clothes – by innocently declaring, 'I've never been alone with a man before, even with my dress on. With my dress off, it's MOST unusual'. With this transformation comes a great sense of freedom and independence:

Princess Ann: I could do some of the things I've always wanted to.
Joe Bradley: Like what?
Princess Ann: Oh, you can't imagine. I'd do just whatever I liked all day long.

As part of her transformation, Ann adopts the enigmatic persona of Anya Smith or 'Smitty' who spends the night in Joe's apartment, cuts off her hair, dresses in those much desired pyjamas, smokes cigarettes, gets into a fight on a barge, causes havoc on the streets of Rome on Joe's scooter, and almost gets arrested by the Roman police force for her erratic driving (with Gregory Peck in Figure 2). In other words, the Princess does everything a princess is not supposed to do – and she revels in it. Costuming is again crucial as Ann undergoes a series of subtle changes to her outfit that results in the creation of Anya. First, she purchases a pair of flat sandals in the market; second, she goes into a barbers and demands that her long hair is cut off; third, she rolls up the sleeves of her semi-formal blouse to give a more casual appearance; and finally, she opens the neck of her blouse and adds a neckerchief to complete her visual transformation.

According to Ian Woodward in his book *Audrey Hepburn: Fair Lady of the Screen*, Hepburn once said, 'If I'm honest I have to tell you I still read fairy tales and I like them best of all', and *Roman Holiday* certainly has some fairy-tale elements such as Anya's lost slipper at the ball, finding her 'Prince Charming' albeit in the form of an 'average Joe', and the 'pumpkin moment' when Anya returns to the palace to transform back into Princess Ann. However, there is no happy ending for the princess as she must lose her 'prince' once she returns to her royal life.

Audrey Hepburn: Fashion, Fairy Tales and Transformation
Lynn Hilditch

Figure 3: Hepburn as the young, lovelorn Sabrina Fairchild in Sabrina.

'Paris is always a good idea' (Sabrina Fairchild, *Sabrina*)

A year later in Billy Wilder's comedy *Sabrina*, Hepburn played another modern-day Cinderella; Sabrina Fairchild, a chauffeur's daughter, who has grown up living above the garage belonging to the wealthy Larrabee family of Long Island. Sabrina is a young, lovelorn girl who dreams of being swept off her feet by her 'prince' in the form of the youngest Larrabee son David (William Holden) – a three-time married playboy who has never given her a second glance. However, after being sent on a trip to Paris by her father to learn how to cook (and, hopefully, to forget David), Sabrina returns home two years later having transformed mentally and physically from the 'scrawny little kid' with her hair in a ponytail and wearing a girlish 'sack-dress' and collarless black shirt (see Figure 3) into a French- speaking, chicly dressed 'sophisticated woman' in a stylish dark two-piece double-breasted suit and accessorizing her stylish Parisian outfit with kitten heels, gloves, a light-coloured turban hat and bohemian-style hoop earrings (see Figure 4). She also has the ultimate French fashion accompaniment – a toy poodle (humorously named David), also exquisitely dressed in a diamante collar. In a letter written to her father a few days before returning from Paris, Sabrina demonstrates how she has considerably matured as she pronounces, 'I have learned how to live; how to be in the

Figure 4: Hepburn as the 'sophisticated woman' after her Parisian transformation in Sabrina.

world and of the world.'

In many of Hepburn's films, including *Funny Face, Love in the Afternoon* (Billy Wilder, 1957), *Charade* (Stanley Donen, 1963), *Paris When It Sizzles* (Richard Quine, 1964), *How to Steal a Million* (William Wyler, 1966) and *Bloodline* (Terence Young, 1979), Paris is the city of ultimate sophistication and life-changing experiences. Sabrina acknowledges Paris's positive role in her transformation in a conversation with the elder Larrabee brother, Linus (Humphrey Bogart):

Sabrina Fairchild: Maybe you should go to Paris, Linus. It helped me. Have you ever been there?
Linus Larrabee: [thinks] Oh yes. Once. For thirty-five minutes.
Sabrina Fairchild: Thirty-five minutes?
Linus Larrabee: Changing planes. I was on my way to Iraq on an oil deal.
Sabrina Fairchild: Oh, but Paris isn't for changing planes, it's for changing your outlook! For throwing open the windows and letting in … letting in *la vie en rose.*

In contrast to *Roman Holiday*, Sabrina is at first a young, inexperienced child who then blossoms into an elegant lady. Once this transformation has occurred, Sabrina becomes instantly attractive to the 'Prince Charming' David who eventually sweeps her off her feet at a family ball (although he loses her to the older, wiser Linus at the end of the film). Hepburn felt, according to Woodward, that she was particularly suited to the role

Audrey Hepburn: Fashion, Fairy Tales and Transformation
Lynn Hilditch

of Sabrina, claiming that her character was 'a dreamer who lived a fairy tale and she was a *romantic*, an incorrigible romantic, which I am. I could never be cynical. I wouldn't dare. I'd roll over and *die* before that'.

'I'm not Holly. I'm not Lula Mae, either. I don't know who I am!' (Holly Golightly, *Breakfast at Tiffany's*)

Perhaps the most iconic of Hepburn's self-invented characters is the madcap New York party girl Holly Golightly in the 1961 comedy *Breakfast at Tiffany's*. With her pearls, swept-up hairdo, ludicrously long cigarette holder and 'little black dress', Hepburn helped to transform Truman Capote's heroine into an American cultural icon who, in turn, transformed Hepburn into a much copied style icon (see Figure 5). However, even Holly has a dual identity. While Holly is perceived by some as a 'phoney' and a gold-digger shamelessly using men for her own gain, she is also the epitome of the 'child-woman' who has never really grown up and been forced to use her body to survive. Again, the costuming demonstrates this contrast in characterization in the 'Moon River' (Henry Mancini, 1961) scene as Holly is transformed from the wacky fashionista into her former persona, Lula Mae Barnes, the Texan Hillbilly who ran away

from home, and subsequently a premature marriage, when she was 14 years old. In this scene, Hepburn, becomes an image of purity in a white baggy sweater, blue jeans and her long hair wrapped in a white head scarf, as she trades in Holly's chic black dresses for a more honest and fresh-faced appearance (see Figure 6). However, rather than emulating the persona of a fairy-tale princess, Holly Golightly is very much a damsel in distress, a 'wild thing', who is finally rescued by her knight in a taxi cab, the penniless writer Paul Varjak (George Peppard).

Fig. 5: Hepburn as the madcap Holly Golightly in Breakfast at Tiffany's.

Fig. 6: Hepburn as her Hillbilly alter-ego Lula Mae Barnes in the 'Moon River' scene in Breakfast at Tiffany's.

'Oh no! You could never make a model out of that. I think my face is perfectly funny!' (Jo Stockton, *Funny Face*)

Unlike Hepburn's characters in *Roman Holiday*, *Sabrina* and *Breakfast at Tiffany's* who are mostly self-transformed, in *Funny Face* and *My Fair Lady* Hepburn's characters are forced to undergo a transformation for the benefit of others – a glossy fashion magazine and phonetic research respectively. However, the Cinderella theme is still evident.

Fig. 7: Hepburn as Jo Stockton the bookworm in Funny
Face.

In Stanley Donen's musical comedy *Funny Face*, Hepburn plays Jo Stockton, a drably dressed, intellectual
bookstore worker who is transformed by fashion photographer Dick Avery (Fred Astaire) from 'that creature
in the book shop' into the 'quality woman' – the epitome
of grace, elegance and pizzazz with beauty as well as intellect. Astaire's character, Dick
Avery, was loosely based on the American fashion and portrait photographer Richard
Avedon who provided some of the portraits in the film, including the high-key portrait
of Hepburn in which only her main features – her eyes, eyebrows, nostrils and lips –
are visible. While Jo describes modelling as a 'synthetic beauty' preferring the natural
beauty of trees, Dick uses his charm and talent as an image-maker to transform the
dowdy bookworm into a stunning 'bird of paradise'. Again, costuming is key in *Funny
Face*, particularly in the musical number 'How Long Has This Been Going On (George
and Ira Gershwin, 1927) when Jo, simply dressed in a plain black shirt, burgundy pencil
skirt, shapeless brown tunic and flat burgundy shoes, dances with a large brightly col-
oured bonnet, highly reminiscent of a little girl who has raided her mother's wardrobe
and dreams of becoming a lady (more similarities with *My Fair Lady*) (see Figure 7).
Hepburn's transformation from the intellectual to the beauty in *Funny Face* was again
emphasized through the use of fashion and costuming by the extreme contrast between the tight black outfit worn in the 'Basal Metabolism' (George and Ira Gershwin,
1927) contemporary dance number and the spectacular Givenchy-designed evening
gowns that aided her transformation into the haute couture fashion model (see Figure
8). Finally, the knee-length wedding dress that she wears at the end of the film, as she
floats down the river with her Dick, signifies a fairy-tale ending for the 'princess' and her
'Prince Charming'.

**'I bet that damn gown doesn't fit. I warned you about those French design-
ers!' (Colonel Pickering, *My Fair Lady*)**

Perhaps the most remarkable of Hepburn's forced identity transformations was as the

Audrey Hepburn: Fashion, Fairy Tales and Transformation
Lynn Hilditch

_Fig. 8: Hepburn as Jo Stock-
ton the 'Quality Woman' in
Funny Face._

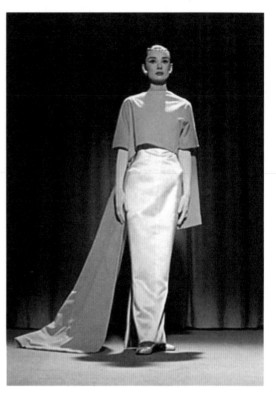

common 'guttersnipe' Eliza Doolittle in George Cukor's musical _My Fair Lady_, based on the 1938 screen adaptation of George Bernard Shaw's 1912 play _Pygmalion_ (see Figure 9). Eliza's transformation occurs when the misogynistic Professor of Phonetics Henry Higgins (Rex Harrison) makes a bet with his scholarly rival Colonel Hugh Pickering (Wilfrid Hyde-White) that he can take a simple Cockney flower girl and pass her off as an aristocrat at a social event. Eliza's incentive for participating in this scheme is the promise of fulfilling her ambition of working as a lady in a flower shop. It might be argued that Hepburn's role as the hungry, dirty-faced flower girl is completely out of character for an actress who was known for her natural style and elegance. However, it might also be argued that Eliza is perhaps the closest the audience gets to meeting the young Edda/Audrey who, as a girl living in Amsterdam during World War II, was close to starvation and forced to scrounge on the streets for food. When Eliza sings the line 'lots of choc-o-late for me to eat' in the 'Wouldn't It Be Loverly' (Frederick Loewe and Alan Jay Lerner, 1956) musical number, the look of joy on Hepburn's face was perhaps reminiscent of the look on the young Edda/Audrey's face when she was given chocolate bars by British airmen after the war. As Hepburn once said, according to Hellstern, being without food and growing up in wartime Europe 'made me resilient and terribly appreciative for everything that came afterward. I felt enormous respect for food, freedom, for good health and family – for human life'. Yet, even as the common flower girl with her 'wretched clothes and dirty face', Hepburn's indisputable grace and good breeding is still evident. Of course, in complete contrast to the flower girl, Hepburn plays the role of the elegant 'lady' to perfection in a series of elaborate costumes designed by the British _Vogue_ photographer and artist Cecil Beaton. As quoted by Hellstern, Hepburn described how she felt when appearing as the 'lady' in the film (see Figure 10):

_Figure 9: Hepburn as the
Cockney flower girl Eliza
Doolittle in My Fair Lady._

In that absolutely sublime dress, with my hair dressed to kill, and diamonds everywhere, I felt super! All I had to do was walk down the staircase in Professor Higgins's house, but the dress made me do it. Clothes, like they say, make the man, but in my case, they also gave me the confidence I often needed.

And, with Eliza's spectacular transformation comes the inevitable attention of a 'Prince Charming' in the form of Freddy Eynsford-Hill (Jeremy Brett), a shallow David Larrabee-type character. However, just like Sabrina Fairchild (with Linus Larrabee)

Fig. 10: Hepburn as the 'lady' in My Fair Lady.

and Jo Stockton (with Dick Avery), Eliza Doolittle chooses to remain with an older and strangely more manipulative and controlling male (Professor Higgins). A father-figure, perhaps, to the little girl who never truly grows up.

While Hepburn could never be described as an 'ugly duckling' or even as 'plain', throughout her films she was able to use effective and creative costuming to enable her to portray characters who assume a sense of the 'ordinary', which is then transformed into something 'extraordinary', or vice versa in the case of *Roman Holiday*. While Hepburn herself never considered herself to be a great beauty and, to some extent, defied what Hollywood considered to be glamorous, she had the ability to transform at will – both on- and off-screen – becoming both waif and woman of the world, friendly and strangely aloof, princess and commoner. While her Hollywood contemporaries triumphed at being curvaceous and sexy, Hepburn was skinny and flat-chested projecting a distinctly child-like, even boyish, appearance – rather like a female Peter Pan (Astaire even croons to Hepburn in the musical number 'Funny Face' (George and Ira Gershwin, 1927), 'You have all the qualities of Peter Pan'). However, it was her natural ability to wear good clothes that made her the envy of women, and with her large, Bambi-like eyes and dazzling smile she made men want to protect her. In addition, the costuming in her films, and her collaborations with Givenchy, Head and Beaton, in particular, helped Hepburn transform her characters into contemporary 'Cinderellas' where dressing up and using fashion for creative effect was a vital part of the acting process. As Hepburn said, as quoted by Hellstern, 'Those movies were fairy tales. That's always been me … I've never changed. A princess or a flower girl were all parts of me and I was parts of them.' ●

Audrey Hepburn: Fashion, Fairy Tales and Transformation
Lynn Hilditch

GO FURTHER

Books

Audrey Hepburn: Fair Lady of the Screen
Ian Woodward
(London: Virgin Books, 1993)

How to be Lovely: The Audrey Hepburn Way of Life
Melissa Hellstern
(London: Robson Books, 2005)

Audrey Style
Pamela Clarke Keogh
(London: Aurum, 2009)

Films

Roman Holiday, William Wyler, dir. (USA: Paramount, 1953)
Sabrina, Billy Wilder, dir. (USA: Paramount, 1954)
Funny Face, Stanley Donen, dir. (USA: Paramount, 1957)
Breakfast at Tiffany's, Blake Edwards, dir. (USA: Paramount, 1961)
My Fair Lady, George Cukor, dir. (USA: Warner Brothers, 1964)

'THOSE MOVIES WERE
FAIRY TALES.
THAT'S ALWAYS BEEN ME...
I'VE NEVER CHANGED.
A PRINCESS OR
A FLOWER GIRL
WERE ALL PARTS OF ME
AND I WAS PART
OF THEM'.

AUDREY HEPBURN

Chapter
2

Audrey Is a
Hep Cat Now

Jacqui Miller

→ The idea for this chapter began a couple of years ago on my birthday. Sitting in my daughter's kitchen, opening my cards, I was ready to be delighted by her choice. However, I was totally unprepared for the thrill that followed when I ripped the flap. Out came a card bearing a photographic image that was simultaneously a pretty cat, Audrey Hepburn and Holly Golightly, in fact, the cat-as-Audrey-as-Holly.

Fig. 1: Those Audrey-cats are everywhere.

What was most charming and remarkable was the fact that although the cat (I would guess a British shorthair silver tabby) had been photoshopped to wear a tiara-adorned brunette chignon hairpiece, 'little black dress' and pearl choker, its beautiful features and delicate markings needed barely any additional 'eye make-up' in order to perfectly replicate Audrey Hepburn's looks. Soon, afterwards, my daughter presented me with a coffee mug adorned with the same image and I found a dress for my granddaughter which did not carry a photographic transfer, but a drawing of a kitten, again wearing a topknot hairpiece and a multi-strand necklace that was palpably obviously a replication of Audrey Hepburn.

A quick trawl on the Internet located numerous items – coasters, luggage tags, key rings and many more, bearing a variant on the photograph/drawing. Of course this is another stage of the cultural proliferation of Audrey Hepburn's star persona, and while that is of interest what fascinated me was the fact that with no written cue needed, a cat could be immediately identified as Audrey Hepburn, a presumption proved many times over when colleagues and students came into my office, saw the card now pinned to the wall and did a double-take: 'that's a cat as Audrey Hepburn'. This made me ponder just how cat-like Audrey Hepburn's image is, and this chapter will explore the context through which this image has been constructed and her various feline layers, from associations from her 'real' life, her 'reel' roles and popular culture, and her fans' interaction with these.

When reading any of the very many Hepburn biographies, one phrase recurs above all others: 'fairy tale'. As a young dancer working on the London stage she opened a Christmas show herself dressed as a fairy complete with wand, whilst it has been said that Audrey's gaining the stage role of Gigi through being spotted as a then unknown young actress in Monte Carlo by the novel's author, Colette, was more akin to a fairy tale than real life. This theme continued throughout her career; films like *Sabrina* (Billy Wilder, 1954) and *My Fair Lady* (George Cukor, 1964) are in a sense modern-day fairy tales as an erstwhile neglected or impoverished girl becomes the belle of the ball – a scenario reversed but achieving the same effect in *Roman Holiday* (William Wyler, 1953). Audrey herself said of her career in films overall, quoted by Donald Spoto: 'If I ever want to accentuate the importance of anything in any form of entertainment, it is the quality of the fairy tale [...] People go to the theatre and the cinema for the same reason that makes them like fairy tales – the sense of watching something that isn't real. The fairy tale is, to my mind, the core of entertainment.'

As well as the rags to riches, transformative aspect to fairy tales, anthropomorphism is often integral, as for example in Cinderella in which mice are turned into horses, a rat into a coachman and lizards become footmen. This anthropomorphism, or at least a close affinity with animals, seems to have formed part of Audrey's childhood. Even her favourite reading included animal tales such as Rudyard Kipling's *The Jungle Book* (1894) and *Just So Stories* (1902) and from an early age, Audrey was known to love ani-

Audrey Is a Hep Cat Now
Jacqui Miller

Fig. 2: 'Don't I count as a woman'? 'No – you're more like a cat!'

mals, preferring them as playmates to dolls. Audrey's household often included a variety of pet animals; while living with her first husband, Mel Ferrer in Vigna San Antonio, Italy, between the filming of *Sabrina* and *War and Peace* (King Vidor, 1956) a menagerie of fan-tailed doves, dogs, a donkey and numerous cats. Indeed, although Audrey's own preference might have been for dogs, she is most closely associated with, and in every way, both physically and spiritually, in her fan's minds, with cats.

Before achieving Hollywood stardom, Audrey had a variety of small parts in British films, including *One Wild Oat* (Charles Saunders, 1951), *Laughter in Paradise* (Mario Zampi, 1951) and *The Lavender Hill Mob* (Charles Crichton, 1951). As is further explored in another chapter in this book, these parts were a rather risqué contrast to the ladylike Hepburn image that would mark her Hollywood work. In each film she played a girl that was essentially an accessory to male extra-curricular dalliance and it is striking that this is aligned to animalistic imagery. *One Wild Oat* is a creaky filmed version of a stage comedy in which Stanley Holloway plays a greyhound trainer who, when his wife thinks she has discovered him in infidelity, claims the female in question is a hound whose sensitivity meant she had to share his hotel room. Audrey plays a hotel receptionist whom we see via a telephone conversation with Holloway. Obviously on intimate terms – he addresses her as 'Honey', before asking if his wife rings up she should tell her that Gloria is a greyhound. When Honey/Gloria reminds him about the registration book, he asks her to add 'bitch' in brackets to the record; a daring double entendre for British cinema in 1951. In *Laughter in Paradise*, a rather more effective ensemble comedy, Audrey plays a cigarette girl who opens with the immortal line: 'Want a ciggy?' Dressed in a style that in the 1960s would be adapted to the 'bunny girl' look, as can be seen from the Figure 2 in an image that will recur throughout a number of her films, Audrey's hair bow is redolent of cat's ears.

The Lavender Hill Mob, a favourite Ealing Comedy, sees Audrey as the 'floozie' of a fraudster-on-the-run played by Alec Guinness. Her part remains tiny, she just appears on-screen to be paid off by cash present presumably for services rendered, but her name is Chiquita; she is a delightful 'chick', again a forerunner of 1960s girls.

It would be Audrey's tiny role in *Laughter in Paradise* that would be instrumental in securing her first starring – and Oscar winning – role, as Princess Ann in *Roman Holiday*. It was at this point in her nascent career that her feline-ness started to attract notice.

Fig. 3: Princess Ann:
A delightful kitten.

Fig. 4: A magical cat – Alice in
Wonderland's Cheshire cat.

Fig. 5: A magical cat –
Sabrina.

Paramount's London production chief had seen *Laughter in Paradise* and arranged a screen test of the scene where the runaway princess wakes up in American journalist Joe Bradley's (Gregory Peck) spare bed. Seeing the footage, one critic describes Audrey as 'stretching in a delightfully kittenish way' and it is this combination of innocence, natural grace and inherent, if unwitting coquetry that would define much of her appeal. During the film, as if in recognition of their shared attributes, a by-standing cat looks on at Ann's nocturnal escapades, but more lasting homage and evidence of a shared love for all things Audrey and feline comes from style blogger Paris Winston's *The Cat's Meow* blog; on 9 July 2012, Paris posted a picture of that day's outfit – a dress and blouse a là Princess Ann.

The success of *Roman Holiday* led to Audrey's next film role, Sabrina Fairchild, a chauffeur's daughter who has a romantic crush on her father's playboy employer, David Larrabee (William Holden) before finding 'grown-up' love with his staid elder brother, Linus (Humphrey Bogart) in *Sabrina*. Reprising the fairy-tale motif of *Roman Holiday*, *Sabrina* again fuses this with Audrey's cat-like literal and metaphorical powers to enchant.

The audience first meets Sabrina at the Larrabee's Long Island estate where they are hosting a society party. Breaking away from helping her father wash one of the Larrabee limousines she climbs a tree barefoot (a familiar escapade for the tomboyish childhood Audrey when playing rough and tumble with her brothers) to survey the glamorous party scene. The camera cross-cuts from Sabrina's longing point-of-view of the guests dancing in evening dress to close-ups of her luminous face as she crouches atop a branch. The film has already begun what is becoming a familiar fairy-tale style for Audrey through Sabrina's opening narration: 'Once upon a time' and in this scene, she evokes one of the characters of Audrey's beloved children's books; the Cheshire Cat in *Alice in Wonderland* (Lewis Carroll, 1865).

This motif is heightened by Sabrina's association with the moon. As the opening credits roll, the visual backdrop to the titles is the Larrabee estate with the moon poised above Hepburn's name, in the next frame forming the dot above the 'i' in 'Sabrina'. When she climbs the tree, she is moonlit, and throughout the film her aspirations are described as 'reaching for the moon'.

Audrey Is a Hep Cat Now
Jacqui Miller

Despite publicity stills prominently featuring Sabrina's post-Parisian fashion transformation in a Givenchy suit accessorized with a French poodle, it is the feline associations, not acknowledged explicitly by the film, that have continued to spark cultural associations and fans' imaginations. The notion of youthful enchantment and mystical powers was enshrined in *Sabrina the Teenage Witch* (Neil Scovell, ABC, 1996-2000), a series which had many proliferations through its original comic book, to the TV shows and the animated prequel. Of course, the family cat, Salem, was an integral character and the lyric to the animated show: 'She's got a superstar cat who knows where it's at' underscores the association. Feline websites today continue to link the two. One fan describes having two cats, one named Sabrina, but the other one having to watch Audrey's *Sabrina* every night before sleep. *Boogipets.com* reports: 'Sabrina. Just like the 50s film featuring Audrey Hepburn, this pet name is pure class!', while *five.pet.place.com* tells of Sabrina (a large tabby) who is 'named after the character in the Audrey Hepburn movie. A very expressive cat, Sabrina has an amazing vocabulary using many different meows, squeaks and purrs to communicate'.

Funny Face (Stanley Donen, 1957) casts Audrey as Jo Stockton, a 'nerdy' Greenwich Village bookstore assistant who is 'discovered' by glossy magazine, *Quality*, as its potential ideal girl. Reluctant to enter the fashion world she despises, Jo is persuaded to go to Paris on a modelling shoot by photographer Dick Avery (Fred Astaire) as a means to meet her idol, an existentialist-style guru of 'epatheticalism'. Like *Sabrina*, *Funny Face* uses Parisian iconography and haute couture, specifically Givenchy designs, as transformative elements in the ongoing Audrey fairy tales. Also, like *Sabrina*, *Funny Face* utilizes a dog to heighten the sophisticated effect, in this case when Jo poses for a high-fashion shot with Audrey's own Yorkshire terrier, Mr Famous. However, it is once again the case that *Funny Face* continues to generate associations with cats amongst Audrey's fandom and cultural reception, even to the extent that its high-fashion origins are left aside. It is recognized within film theory that audiences often 'blank out' a film's ending and narrative trajectory, focusing instead on a key scene that has most meaning for them. Certainly the standout scenes within *Funny Face* are not the fashion shoots and especially not the ersatz closing 'wedding' scene, but those when Jo is in her natural beatnik uniform of cropped trousers, turtleneck sweater and loafers, all in black, but softened by a glimpse of white socks. She truly comes to life in the empatheticalist coffee bar, her dance replicating the free-wheeling prancing and leaping of a cat out on the tiles. Audrey and director Stanley Donen had disagreed about the socks – Audrey felt her costume should be unrelieved black, but Donen insisted on white to draw attention to her dance moves. After filming, Audrey agreed with him, but the white socks have a further effect; to soften a black panther into a kitten, more in keeping with Audrey's persona. However, the film's publicity posters replace the white socks with black, and an altogether more 'edgy' cat is revealed. The tagline, used as the title of this chapter, describes: 'Audrey is a hep-cat now', but it could have read 'now and forever' as this im-

Fig. 6: Audrey is a hep cat now!

Fig. 6: Audrey is a hep cat now!

age continues to define both the essence of the 'beats' and cool contemporary fashion. *Nostalgia Central* website says of the beatnik era: 'Audrey Hepburn's hepcat hipness in *Funny Face* was unforgettable: gamine haircut, black leotard and Capri leggings with ballerina flats' while current fashion blog *Zimbio* describes a recent outfit worn by actress Jennifer Connolly as 'something wonderfully beatnik hepcat meets Audrey Hepburn in *Funny Face*'.

Although three other films (*Love in the Afternoon* [Billy Wilder, 1957], *Green Mansions* [Mel Ferrer, 1959], and *The Nun's Story* [Fred Zinnemann, 1959]) intervened, *Funny Face* was a perfect precursor for *Breakfast at Tiffany's*, the movie which gave Audrey probably the defining character of her star persona, Holly Golightly, the sexy-classy but vulnerable New York good-time girl who eventually finds love with Paul Varjak (George Peppard) the young author living in the same brownstone – as well as being the film which indelibly tied that persona to cats.

At this stage in her career, Audrey realized that she was becoming too old to continue to play the ingénue and moreover, by 1961, on the verge of the 'Swinging Sixties', society had changed; she needed a 'grown-up' role, and one more in keeping with current mores. Although Audrey had reservations about taking the apparently amoral role of Holly, she was persuaded by her agent that Holly was a 'kook', a kind of 'beat-girl'. Being a 'hep cat' was intrinsic to being 'kooky', characteristics already associated with Audrey through *Funny Face*. She drew on its connotations when writing to *Tiffany's* composer, Henry Mancini, describing him as 'the hippest of cats'. The link with *Funny Face*, hip cats and Mancini would become yet tighter in 1963 with the release of *Tiffany's* director, Blake Edwards's *The Pink Panther*, also scored by Mancini. This film introduced the decidedly cool animated pink panther who went on to have his own TV show. This cat was exactly the same colour used to illustrate the *Funny Face* number 'Think Pink' (Roger Edens, 1957) and the film and song were evoked by the 1977–78 series, entitled *Think Pink Panther* (David H. DePatie and Fritz Freleng, NBC, 1977-78). Cats are a metaphorical theme throughout *Tiffany's*. Paul's volume of stories is entitled 'Nine Lives', while Holly steals a cat mask from the five and dime. This association with cats represents Holly's 'kookiness'; her Bohemian free-spirit that cannot be pinned down, something she herself sums up: 'I'm not Holly! I'm not Lula Mae either. I don't know who I am. I'm like Cat here. We're a couple of no-name slobs. We belong to nobody', an idea empha-

Audrey Is a Hep Cat Now
Jacqui Miller

sized by Holly's association, not only with a cat, but a mask, which she implicitly wears long after discarding the artefact.

The publicity poster for *Tiffany's*, and still the most frequently used image associated with the film, represents the duality of Audrey's 'class' and Holly's deviance by fusing haute couture with an alley cat. A drawing rather than a photograph, the image adds curve's to Audrey's slender frame and shows glimpses of thigh peeping from a black Givenchy gown and has Holly's cat (looking far more piratical than the film's Cat) on her shoulder. At a time when stars such as Marilyn Monroe and Jayne Mansfield exhibited images that couldn't possibly be replicated by the average young woman, Holly's style immediately made high fashion and movie-star style potentially accessible. This is surely why Audrey continues to be a style guru for the modern woman long after Monroe's theatrical style has been relegated to parody and fancy dress.

As I noted at the beginning of this chapter, Audrey's feline-ness has been enshrined by the vast range of commodities merging Audrey-with-Holly-with-a-cat, whose eyes barely need enhancement to capture her look. It is often her cat-like eyes which represent the essence of Audrey for her fans. Along with the little black dress, one of the iconic items in *Tiffany's* is Holly's large-framed sunglasses, dubbed 'cat-eye' sunglasses. Featured on every 'get the Audrey look' fashion blog, such as *Stylelist*, these frames, now made by designers such as Tom Ford, are worn by modern stars including Jennifer Lopez, Selma Hayek and Dita von Teese, seeking to draw on Audrey's timeless chic. The 'Audrey Hepburn cat eye' has entered fashion parlance as shorthand for a classic style involving black eyeliner, and fashion magazines regularly demonstrate products and techniques to use. Were this not enough, bloggers such as Kandee Johnson offer online step-by-step advice on 'How to – Audrey Make-Up – glam cat eyeliner'. At the time of writing, Audrey's feline elegance with its hint of elegant sexuality is causing a new furore with the release of Christopher Nolan's *The Dark Knight Rises* (2012). In one scene Selina Kyle (Anne Hathaway) wears an almost identical costume to one of Holly Golightly's, and as a jewel thief presumably loves Tiffany's just as much. More importantly, though, Selina is Catwoman, a cat-woman, who, through her identification with the comic-book incarnation is closely drawn from Audrey. As Adam Hughes, artist of the *Catwoman* comic covers from 1980 to 1985 said of his inspiration in an interview with Jon Gordon:

For the longest time I played around asking 'Who is Selina Kyle, what is she like?' And then I realized I really liked the 1950s and 1960s *To Catch a Thief* lounge-apartment type of feel. And at one point I just went 'That's her!' She is this kind of 1950s Audrey Hepburn kind of character with way too much eyebrow make-up and short black hair. And I went 'Perfect! That is it!' And from then on it wasn't just about the face, but I had a great idea of who the character was.

This has led fans such as blogger tsukarera on WordPress to ponder 'Why does Catwoman look like Audrey Hepburn?' while discussion on LiveJournal's *Saving People* caused fans to go back and not just revisit *Breakfast at Tiffany's* but to uncover a whole stream of forgotten Audrey/Catwoman references, such as the fact that Holly Robinson with the nickname '*Go-Nightly*' took over the Catwoman role for a while. One thing is certain: Audrey's association with cats has far more than nine lives! ●

Audrey Is a Hep Cat Now
Jacqui Miller

~~~~~~~~~~~~~~

GO FURTHER

Books

Enchantment: The Life of Audrey Hepburn
Donald Spoto
(London: Hutchinson, 2006)

Films

Alice in Wonderland, Tim Burton, dir. (United States/United Kingdom: Roth Films/
Team Todd/Tim Burton Productions/The Zanuck Company, 2010)
The Pink Panther, Blake Edwards, dir. (United States: The Mirisch Company, 1963)

Online

The Cat's Meow [Blogspot], http://pariswinston.blogspot.co.uk/2012/07/roman-
holiday.html

'Sabrina'. *Five Pet Place* [n.d.], https://www.fivepetplace.com/p/sabrina

'Best Classic, Romantic Movie: Sabrina'. *Yahoo! Voices*, 15 April 2008, http://voices.
yahoo.com/best-classic-romantic-movie-sabrina-3075388.html?cat=40.
Stylist.co.uk

'Why it Works: Jennifer Connely'
Kristina D. Swift
Zimbio. 13 June 2012, http://www.zimbio.com/Jennifer+Connelly/articles/
VZsLNat5Enp/Why+it+Works+Jennifer+Connelly.
Boogiepets.com Thoughts
Boogiepets.com.4 November 2013,
http://www.boogiepets.com/pet.php?name=Sabrina

Cat Eye Sunglasses: Audrey Hepburn, Jennifer Lopez, Deeta Von Teese & More Love
this Eyewear'
Sarah Leon
Huffington Post. 7 March 2012,
http://www.huffingtonpost.com/2012/07/03/cat-eye-sunglasses-celebrity_n_1644221.
html

Kandee Johnson, http://www.kandeej.com/

'Why does Catwoman look like Audrey Hepburn?'
tsukareru (pseud.)
Tsukareru [WordPress]. 22 February 2011, http://tsukareru.wordpress.com/2011/02/22/why-does-catwoman-look-like-audrey-hepburn/

'The Audrey Hepburn Connections to the Dark Knight Rises'
Saving People [LiveJournal]. 30 June 2012, http://savingpeople.livejournal.com/435813.html.
'Arkham City: Why Catwoman looks like Audrey Hepburn'
Jon Gordon
Play Magazine. 4 November 2011, http://www.play-mag.co.uk/general/why-catwoman-looks-like-audrey-hepburn/

Chapter 3

Why is Hepburn so 'Audrey'?

Esperanza Miyake

→ Her doe-eyed smile. The elfin face. A swan-like neck braced with a string of pearls, a balletic figure poised with grace and decorum. We as audiences, photographers, journalists, fashionistas and fans cannot help but gather around her with admiration, adoration and endless fascination.

Fig. 1: In the words of Henry Higgins (Rex Harrison), 'If I were a woman who'd been to a ball, been hailed as a princess by one and by all'.

Hepburn was Hollywood royalty in all senses of the word: think of her Academy-award winning role as Princess Ann in the film, *Roman Holiday* (William Wyler, 1953); her real-life aristocratic lineage; her status as a screen icon amongst the Hollywood elite. She was, and still remains, regal.

Throughout her acting career, Hepburn has played very different roles: a nun (*The Nun's Story* [Fred Zinnemann, 1959]); a society 'it' girl (*Breakfast at Tiffany's* [Blake Edwards, 1961]); a criminal (*How to Steal a Million* [William Wyler, 1966]); a blind woman (*Wait Until Dark* [Terence Young, 1967]); and Robin Hood's Lady Marian (*Robin and Marian* [Richard Lester, 1976]) to name a few. For me, part of the delight in watching Hepburn is that throughout all these various roles, she seems to always retain her 'essence', a certain Audrey-ness, no matter what her character or appearance may be: always elegant, touched with a humble and delicate sense of refinement. Such reasons make Hepburn's role as a cockney flower girl (Eliza Doolittle) in the musical film *My Fair Lady* (George Cukor, 1964) even more fascinating to me, precisely because she seems to embody – at least in the beginning of the film – antithetic qualities which we do not usually associate with her. Eliza at the beginning is a dirty, working-class girl selling flowers on the street. By the end of the film, Eliza is transformed into an articulate, middle-class/upper-class Lady, mistaken for Hungarian royalty: much closer to the 'essence' of Audrey.

But what exactly *is* this 'essence', the certain ethereal and ephemeral quality of Audrey that is at once both subtle and sublime, yet intoxicating and powerfully present? The answer to this question for me has always been as clear as the crystals of a chandelier cascading down towards a majestic Hepburn: *her voice; her posture; and her playfulness*. These three notes for me compose the beautiful melody that is Audrey, a symphony of sound, image and character. Like a listener attempting to understand the complexities of a piece of music, I want to look these three notes through Hepburn/ Eliza both at the beginning and end of *My Fair Lady* to understand and explain what I feel is the 'essence' of Audrey.

'Well, you have my voice on your gramophone. When you feel lonely without me you can turn it on' (Eliza Doolittle)

Based on George Bernard Shaw's *Pygmalion* (1912), the musical follows the story of Eliza Doolittle whose speech and thus manner are reformed by a rich bachelor and phonetics professor (Henry Higgins/Rex Harrison) so she may 'pass' as royalty. We are first introduced to Eliza Doolittle as a loud and loquacious flower girl whose sound and accent offend yet interest Professor Higgins. The stage directions describe Eliza as 'wailing',

Why is Hepburn so 'Audrey'?
Esperanza Miyake

Fig. 2: Eliza is described by Higgins as a 'bilious pigeon' and a 'pris'ner of the gutters' who should be 'taken out and hung for the cold-blooded murder of the English tongue'

'hysterical', 'crying wildly' throughout this opening sequence and in fact, despite being so talkative, Eliza is an uncontrollable cacophony of shrill, non-verbal sounds. Even the very first word we hear her utter in the film is, 'Aaaaaooww', a caterwauling aimed at a gentleman (Freddy, later to be her admirer) who accidentally pushes her over.

> Higgins: A woman who utters such depressing and disgusting sounds has no right to be anywhere – no right to live. Remember that you are a human being with a soul and the divine gift of articulate speech; that your native language is the language of Shakespeare and Milton and the Bible; and don't sit there crooning like a bilious pigeon.
> Eliza: (*Quite overwhelmed, looking up at him in mingled wonder and deprecation without daring to raise her head*) Aoooooooooooowl.
> Higgins: Look at her – a pris'ner of the gutters; Condemned by ev'ry syllable she utters. By right she should be taken out and hung for the cold-blooded murder of the English tongue.
> Eliza: A-o-o-o-wl.
> Higgins: (*Imitating her*) Aoooow! Heavens, what a noise!

Higgins's task (or bet with Colonel Pickering) is to teach Eliza how to contain and control the feral 'depressing and disgusting sounds' leaking out of this 'bilious pigeon', to 'liberate' her from the 'prison of the gutter', to transform both her appearance and behaviour by enabling her to master 'the English tongue'. This means she must not only learn how to *sound* genteel, she must also learn how to *speak* and pronounce her words correctly – particularly her vowels and 'h's in order to mask her cockney origins.

> Aoooow! One would think you was my father!
> Higgins: If I decide to teach you, I'll be worse than two fathers to you. Here. (*He offers her his silk handkerchief*)
> Eliza: What's this for?
> Higgins: To wipe your eyes. To wipe any part of your face that feels moist. Remember, that's your handkerchief; and that's your sleeve. Don't mistake the one for the other if you wish to become a lady in a shop.

Surely enough, despite a 'slippage' at Ascot when she instinctively reverts back to her old self both in sound and accent,[1] by the end of the film, Eliza becomes a softly spo-

Fig. 3: Eliza's outburst leads to Higgins giving her a handkerchief…and instructing her on its use.

Fig. 4: Hepburn and melancholia, a bitter-sweet beauty that touches the soul.

ken, articulate Lady who can even fool the rather sly and vulpine linguist, Zoltan Karpathy. The voice of the new Eliza is whispery and even a little hoarse, measured yet mellifluous: for me, *this* is the sound of Audrey. Think of Hepburn singing 'Moon River' in *Breakfast at Tiffany's*, there is an almost melodious atonality, a coarse texture to her voice which submerges the tune in deep melancholia and pathos. Audrey's voice has always been rich with poignancy for me, a quiet yet lively sound tinged with a taste of sadness. That is why in *My Fair Lady*, when Marni Nixon's clean and clear voice suddenly flows out Hepburn's/Eliza's mouth,[2] I encounter a moment of aural disorientation – akin to the Ascot scene where sound and vision of Eliza do not match – where the film's emotional tone alter for the duration of a given song. Audrey's voice is pitched right between happiness and sadness, a vocal 'essence' that tastes bitter-sweet to our ears.

Some people say that foreigners make the best language teachers. A daughter of a Dutch Baroness and a British Austrian businessman, Hepburn was born in Belgium, held British citizenship, and could speak English, Dutch, French, Spanish and Italian fluently. The fact that she plays the role of a shrieking, working-class 'guttersnipe' who 'murders the English tongue' is very ironical indeed. But perhaps it takes an actress with such linguistic dexterity in real life to play the role of someone lacking verbal style. Eliza's accent at the end is closer to the Audrey we hear in interviews and other films: clipped, clear and well-enunciated. Within Hollywood and amongst her contemporaries, Hepburn's European status and oddly non-English English – a European English perhaps – has always marked her out. For me, it is Hepburn's accent, as much as the texture of her voice that makes her distinctly Audrey, a sonorous 'essence' that echoes within us.

I could have danced all night!

> Higgins: Yes, you squashed cabbage leaf, you disgrace to the noble architecture of these columns, you incarnate insult to the English language.

As if to point towards the 'gutter where she belongs', Eliza's body at the beginning of *My Fair Lady* is a misshapen bundle of rags, hunched over, stooped low as if weighed down by the bird's-nest mass of hair from under which she peers out with suspicious and beady eyes. Eliza's back is bent, like a Quasimodo of Covent Garden, hobbling like a witch selling charms hidden in her over-sized basket which emphasizes her penuriously skinny body. Higgins describes her aptly if not somewhat cruelly as a 'squashed cabbage'. Eliza's demeanour and posture are indeed weak, quite unlike 'the noble architecture of these columns' (Higgins). Eliza is thus ostensibly shorter than Higgins and Pickering at the beginning of the film, an indication of her inferiority in both class and self-assurance.

Why is Hepburn so 'Audrey'?
Esperanza Miyake

Fig. 5: Higgins calls Eliza a 'disgrace to the noble archi-tecture of these columns'.

Like the evolution of mankind, by the end of the film, Eliza's back is straight – if not straighter than Higgins's – she no longer hobbles and grovels along the cobble stones, her chin is held high with pride and confidence. The new Eliza stands tall, as tall as Higgins who no longer poses such a daunting figure to her. Once an insubstantial 'squashed cabbage', the transformed Eliza is now a 'tower of strength', imposing despite her delicate physique, ready to meet the challenges of another man. Eliza's posture towards the end of the film – particularly during the Royal Ball and her final confrontation with Higgins at Mrs Higgins's house – belongs unmistakeably to Audrey. Proud, majestic and glorious but never arrogant or over-confident. Always modest and humble, whilst being as magnificent as a Greek column.

Hepburn began ballet lessons when she was 6 years old, and continued her training throughout most of her adolescence. Unsurprisingly, in her first major role as Nora Brentano, a ballerina in *The Secret People* (Sidney Cole, 1952), Hepburn's dancing skills are clearly used: 'she's enchanting,' are the words used to describe her even back then. Again, it would take someone with such physical dexterity and finesse to play a role of Eliza, whose body and mien change slowly and subtly over time. It is Hepburn's posture, the connection between her back

and her neck that makes her Audrey in any film, dancing or no dancing. Hepburn's silhouette can be drawn in a single, masterful brush-stroke: smooth and linear, slim and sleek, beautiful and breathtaking. It is no wonder Hepburn became such a muse who inspired French designer, Hubert de Givenchy. For me, part of Audrey's sophistication and elegance – her visual and structural 'essence' – lie precisely in her movements, her ability to make clothes look good, the manner in which she simply walks across a room as if she were dancing amongst the stars, gliding across the screen like a beautiful silver swan.

Fig. 6 (above): No longer a 'disgrace to the noble architecture', Eliza is now a 'tower of strength, a consort battleship!'

Fig. 7 (above left): A breathtaken Freddy expresses our own thoughts, 'She was magnificent!'.

As Eliza spins out her daydream...
In many ways, *My Fair Lady* is a story about transformation. From poor to rich, dirty to clean, working class to upper class, gutter to home; we watch Eliza as she negotiates her way through these various processes of change. One of the most important – if not the most subtle – metamorphoses is Eliza's journey between girlhood and womanhood: from flower *girl* to a fair *Lady*. One of the scenes where Eliza's childlike wonder shines like a twinkling star is when she sings the song, 'Wouldn't it be Lovely?' (Frederick Leowe and Alan Jay Lerner, 1956) along with the costermongers in Covent Garden. Like a girl playing make-believe, she daydreams of a better life which includes eating 'lots of choc'late'. As Eliza sings, 'Someone's head restin' on my knee / Warm and tender as he

*Fig. 8 – 11: Hepburn's playful-
ness is contagious when she
sings and dances to 'Wouldn't
it be Loverly?'*

can be / Who takes good care of me / Oh, wouldn't it be loverly?', there is something
very innocent in her desire to simply be warm, fed and comforted like a child with no
worries or cares of the world. Eliza is also genuinely playful during the song, her eyes are
wide and excited, like a child looking into an invisible window-shop full of fantasies and
dreams. She dances with over-exaggerated and comical movements, and her parodical
parade up a cart-full of cabbages using a cabbage leaf as a fan both mocks and yearns
the existence of those higher up in society.

> All I want is a room somewhere,
> Far away from the cold night air;
> With one enormous chair ...
> Oh, wouldn't it be loverly?
>
> Lots of choc'late for me to eat;
> Lots of coal makin' lots of heat;
> Warm face, warm hands, warm feet ...
> Oh, wouldn't it be loverly?
>
> Someone's head restin' on my knee,
> Warm and tender as he can be,
> Who takes good care of me ...
> Oh, wouldn't it be loverly?
>
> (*When she finishes, the four at the fire beguiled into the mood repeat the refrain as
> ELIZA and the others act out a dinner in an expensive restaurant: the ordering, the
> wine, the food and riding home in a taxi afterwards. A dustcart serves the purpose.*)

Eliza's childlike quality is reinforced when she moves into Higgins's house. An avuncu-
lar Pickering questions Higgins's intentions ('I shall feel responsible for the girl. I hope
it's clearly understood that no advantage is to be taken of her position'), and Higgins's
response ('What? That thing? Sacred, I assure you') strips Eliza of any sexuality. Eliza
herself even states, 'One would think you was my father!' Even Mrs Pearce, the house-
keeper, acts as a sensible, stern yet kindly mother-figure who ensures Eliza is comfort-
able, at times against Higgins's orders. The entire household thus have a protective and
parental concern over Eliza.

> Mrs Pearce: You've all been working much too hard. I think the strain is beginning
> to show. Eliza, I don't care what Mr Higgins says, you must put down your books and
> go to bed.

Why is Hepburn so 'Audrey'?
Esperanza Miyake

Fig. 12: A concerned Mrs. Pearce insists on putting the dreamy Eliza to bed.

Towards the end of *My Fair Lady*, having gone through the symbolic rite of passage during 'The Rain in Spain' where she first succeeds in pronouncing her vowels correctly, Eliza loses some of her childlike and even childish playfulness. Eliza turns into a woman, a Lady who can control herself, her tongue and be responsible for her status and bearing. Just before Eliza, Higgins and Pickering leave for the Royal Ball, Higgins sneaks in a quick glass of port – unseen by Pickering – suggesting his nervous excitement after seeing Eliza for the first time in her full-grown splendour. This incident suggests that Eliza is suddenly seen for the first time as a potential mate, no longer an asexual child-like street urchin under his care.

Yet despite the fair Lady's maturity, the very last words Eliza utters in the film are again, playful. Having momentarily fled unhappily from Higgins's house, Eliza purposely reverts back to her cockney accent just to surprise Higgins and mark her return: 'I washed my face and hands before I come, I did,' she states, the exact same sentence she used when she first set foot in Higgins's house. This moment captures Audrey's unique femininity, which for me is underlined by a whimsical playfulness: sometimes it makes her innocently girl-like, cheeky and cute; yet at other times, it turns into something more mature, coy and flirtatious. Sometimes, and I feel this very last scene in *My Fair Lady* is a good example, she can be both at the same time: cute and beautiful; innocent yet knowingly wise. Hepburn's mischievousness is I feel, the 'essence' of her femininity and attraction. Perhaps this is the reason why so many have described her as being 'elfin'.

I want to conclude by returning to my initial statement. Audrey Hepburn was, and still remains, regal. Divine. Whilst I have tried to explore the 'essence' of Audrey specifically through her voice, posture and playfulness as Eliza in *My Fair Lady*, I know that I have not done Hepburn justice. Like the scent of a blossoming flower, Hepburn's 'essence' is something so natural, so subtle and so profound that it can never be – never should be? – captured or bottled away by an explanation. Perhaps, herein lies Hepburn's essential charm: she is, quite simply, undefinable. ●

Fig. 13: Woman and girl: that cheeky smile that is so 'Audrey'.

NOTES

Endnotes

1 The stage directions for this scene are as follows: ELIZA: (*Her voice crescendoes. The LADIES and GENTLEMEN move perceptively away from this ugly exhibition of natural behaviour*) Come on, Dover!!! Move your bloomin' arse!!! (*An agonizing moan rises up from the crowd. The moment she says it she realizes what she has done and brings her hand to her mouth as if trying to push the words back in. Several women gracefully faint, and are caught by their escorts. LORD and LADY BOXINGTON are staggered. PICKERING flies from the scene running faster than Dover. HIGGINS, of course, roars with laughter*)

2 Often criticized for her supposed inability to sing, Hepburn's singing voice was deemed unsuitable by the producers of My Fair Lady for singing the songs in the film, thus Nixon's voice was dubbed over Hepburn's.

Chapter
4

Transformation, Fashion and Funny Face

Claire Molloy

→ Will: Hey, sweetie! Ah, you brought lunch. Yay! Love the outfit: Very Audrey Hepburn.
Grace: Great. So you're saying I have the neck of a swan and the chest of a 12-year-old boy.
Will: Hey! Way to snatch an insult out of the jaws of a compliment.
Grace: It's a gift.
(*Will and Grace*, Season 1, Episode 8)

Figure 1: Grace arrives at Will's office dressed in black.

Fig. 2: In Funny Face Hepburn dances to jazz in the Parisian cafe.

Fig. 3: Sabrina visits Linus in Sabrina.

Arguably, the black cigarette pants, sweater and flat pumps – the outfit referenced in an episode of *Will and Grace*, entitled 'The Buying Game' – is one of Hepburn's best known 'looks', worn during the expressive dance scene in the bohemian Parisian cafe in *Funny Face* (Stanley Donen, 1957) (see Figure 2) and, in another variation with a daring v-back top (see Figure 3), when she visits Linus in *Sabrina* (Billy Wilder, 1954).

Indeed, the black skinny pants outfit is eclipsed, in terms of its iconic status in the popular consciousness, only by the 'little black dress' made famous by Hepburn in *Breakfast at Tiffany's* (Blake Edwards, 1961). A version of Hepburn's *Funny Face* outfit is worn by Beyoncé during the 2011 video for 'Countdown' in which the singer plays tribute to the dance sequence, using elements of the number combined with references to Diana Ross and the Supremes, Brigitte Bardot, Andy Warhol, Twiggy and the work of Belgian choreographer, Anna Teresa De Keersmaeker. And, before Beyoncé's 'Countdown', the video for Whitney Houston's 1990 hit 'I'm Your Baby Tonight' also borrowed from Hepburn's *Funny Face* performance, somewhat coincidently mixing it with references to Diana Ross and the Supremes, and recreating aspects of Marlene Dietrich's performance, with Houston wearing a white suit and hat, from *Morocco* (Joseph von Sternberg, 1930). Such references underline the resonance that Hepburn's black-pants outfit and *Funny Face* performance have within popular culture.

In the 1950s, images of Hepburn wearing trousers reached audiences long before they saw her don the black Givenchy pants for *Funny Face*. While Dietrich had caused a sensation in 1930s Hollywood wearing men's clothes, Hepburn was at the forefront of the change in women's fashion, popularizing trousers and establishing them as acceptable garments for the female wardrobe. It was therefore not a shock to see, across Europe and the United States, publicity for *Funny Face* that depicted Hepburn in cigarette pants, black turtleneck sweater and flat pumps, eyes closed, heels lifted off the ground, knees slightly bent, hands thrust high above her head, captured executing one of the expressive dance moves from the film.

A close-up of Hepburn's face and a much smaller image of her co-star, Fred Astaire, also caught in the throes of a dynamic dance pose, were the other main elements in the French, Spanish, British and American film posters. In some versions, the poster included two additional images of Hepburn in mid-dance that, in conjunction with the larger central image, suggested that the film included a range of styles: modern, tap, chorus line and ballet. The posters gave no indication, however, that *Funny Face* was a film about fashion and the fashion industry. In fact, the arrangement of elements in the posters suggested that the film was more concerned with dance than couture and, moreover, because the two stars were shown executing solitary dance steps, there was no visual reference made to the romance which blossoms between Hepburn's and Astaire's characters on-screen. Lacking imagery of the couple dancing together or in each other's arms, the largest and most striking element in most versions of the poster was the angular Hepburn pose; her slender outline silhouette-like thanks to the all-black outfit which would come to be so

Transformation, Fashion and Funny Face
Claire Molloy

Fig. 4: Hepburn depicted in an angular dance pose in a poster for Funny Face.

widely referenced in popular culture many decades later.

In 2006, thirteen years after Hepburn's death, the outfit she wore in the film received widespread public attention when clothing retailer Gap used the dance sequence from *Funny Face* in a marketing campaign for a re-launch of 'the perfect black pant'. In doing this, Gap followed a trend for using dead film stars to market commercial products, harnessing, as other companies had done before them, the celebrity brand power of stars such as Marilyn Monroe, Elvis Presley, John Wayne, Fred Astaire, Gene Kelly and Steve McQueen. To get some sense of the success of this strategy, it is worth considering that in 2009, the revenue generated by dead stars in North America totalled $2.25 billion and such is the extent of the business in licensing rights by the estates of dead stars, that the deals are reported annually in the Forbes Top-Earning Dead Celebrities List. In 2006, critical reception of the Gap advertisement was mixed, however, with a number of commentators claiming that, in an era of dead celebrity product endorsement, the commercial use of Hepburn's image had gone a step too far. A report from the *Huffington Post* referred to the advert as 'crass',

Figure 5: Hepburn appears to step from the original *Funny Face* footage into the Gap advert.

Miller describing his reaction to it in the following way: 'I just saw the new Gap commercial featuring Audrey Hepburn and my mouth is frozen in a silent scream.' An NBCNews report summed-up the reaction of many Hepburn fans to the advert: 'I love Hepburn, she feels like too cherished an icon to be hawking clothes.' (NBCNews.com, 6 October 2006)

Yet, even those reports which criticized Gap for its use of Hepburn's image made mention of the advertisement's technical achievements. With the benefits of CGI at their disposal, the advert begins with footage of Hepburn in the bohemian cafe in *Funny Face*. Hepburn delivers the line 'I rather feel like expressing myself now and I could certainly use a release', throws her hands above her head and then appears to high-step from the *Funny Face* footage into the Gap advertisement to the strains of the AC/DC track, 'Back in Black' (1981). Some of Hepburn's original lines from the film are sampled while the dance routine is edited to emphasize the most exuberant movements; those that Richard Dyer has referred to, in his 1985 essay 'Entertainment and Utopia' as the 'show biz elements' such as the 'use of syncopated clapping, forming a vaudeville line-up and American ballet shapes'. Against a plain background that is the colour of classic Gap khaki, imagery of the star dancing is mirrored then duplicated across the screen, at times repeated to produce a kaleidoscope effect. Stars-and-stripes motifs emerge, punctuating Hepburn's dance moves and forming patterned areas which she appears to step on to. Coupled with close-up shots of Hepburn smiling, the overall effect is one of blissful play; a feeling somewhat removed from that of the original film with its mix of modern dance elements choreo-graphed by Eugene Loring and performed to a piece of free-form jazz-inspired music played in a dimly lit meeting place for Left Bank French intellectuals. The original context is stripped away for the majority of the advert although Hepburn eventually returns to the film footage at the commercial's conclusion. As she appears to leap back into the original footage, Brian Johnson sings 'Well I'm back in black / Yes I'm back in black' and the advert ends with the tagline 'It's back: The skinny black pant'.

Gap chose to name the 'skinny black pant' the Audrey Hepburn™ Pant. In a 2006 press statement about Gap's new 'Keep it Simple' campaign the vice president of marketing was quoted, saying, 'This ad is a true testament to timeless style and we couldn't be more excited to have Audrey Hepburn – the ultimate style icon – represented in our campaign.' By wearing the slim-fitting pants, flat shoes and black top in *Funny Face* and in the earlier film *Sabrina*, Hepburn had popularized the look decades before. However, in *Funny Face* Hepburn's character, Jo Stockton, is a follower of 'empathicalism', a philosophy based on empathy for others, who refers to fashion magazines as 'chi-chi and an unrealistic ap-proach to self-impressions'. The bohemian dance she performs is Jo's moment of self-expression, apparently freed from the constraints of the superficial world of fashion she purports to dislike so much. In this way, *Funny Face* gently satirizes the world of fashion, beatniks and existentialism, while the black outfit Hepburn wears is meant to symbolize her character's rejection of fashion. Despite its original narrative context, this particular outfit has acquired popular cultural meanings which reference, instead, Hepburn's as-sociation with couture styling and her background in ballet. In her 2002 book *Growing Up With Audrey Hepburn: Text, Audience, Resonance*, Rachael Moseley has traced these associations to the 1950s noting that any reservations about a perceived shift in women adopting trousers as part of their everyday wardrobe, considered at the time to be mascu-line garments, were allayed by the association between certain styles of pants and dance, in particular ballet. Moseley comments that in the 1950s: 'Audrey Hepburn's trouser wear-ing [was] made acceptable through a relation to dance as an appropriately feminine mode of movement'. Moreover, Hepburn was credited by the popular press for singlehandedly elevating the ballet slipper to the status of a style statement.

By 1954 Hepburn, following her appearance in *Roman Holiday* (William Wyler, 1953), had become a sensation and it was reported that, due to her popularizing them, annual sales of ballet slippers had grown to 1.5 million. Indeed, such was Hepburn's appeal that Lowry wrote in 1954 that simply having a picture of the 'new Hepburn' on the front cover of a magazine 'is like a Benzedrine pill to sales'. Hepburn's association with ballet was fre-quently discussed in the press where it was noted that the star's body was unlike that of her peers. At a time when the curvy hourglass figure was idealized, Hepburn was described as slim or gamine, with a tiny waist (reportedly a mere 20½ inches), and having the body of a dancer. Such descriptions were however concerned primarily with the aesthetics of her body rather than a reference to any talent she possessed as a dancer. This was reflected in

Transformation, Fashion and Funny Face
Claire Molloy

.

reviews of *Funny Face*, when upon its release, some film critics suggested that audiences might find Hepburn's performance unexpected. In 1957 Monahan noted, 'This is the first song-dance role on film for Miss Hepburn and she is a definite surprise' and another commented in *Milwaukee Journal*, 'Audrey's dancing may come as a surprise, but she keeps in perfect step with Astaire, who is at his elegant best'. Hepburn's femininity, the unusualness (for Hollywood) of her body type and the construction of the 'Hepburn style' were understood through references to ballet with its connotations of elegance, grace and – due to repeated references to her 'dance and musical training overseas' – European culture. By teaming Hepburn with Astaire for *Funny Face*, a dance film about fashion, all the key aspects of Hepburn's star persona could be exploited.

In the television series, *Will and Grace* (Kohan & Mutchnick, NBC, 1998-2006), the reference to Hepburn and her skinny black pants outfit provides material for humour familiar to regular viewers of the series; that is, jokes that rely on allusions to Grace's 'flat boyish chest' and the importance of designer fashion to gay culture. In addition to Judy Garland, Bette Davis, Katherine Hepburn and Elizabeth Taylor – actresses referred to elsewhere in the series as gay icons – Audrey Hepburn is also acknowledged as part of gay culture during multiple episodes of *Will and Grace*. However, the references to Hepburn revolve primarily around style and narratives of transformation made possible by fashion. The main elements of humour in the *Will and Grace* scene described at the opening to this chapter – the gamine body and a stylish fashion sense – collide in one of the well-known stories about Hepburn and her association with fashion designer Hubert de Givenchy. Indeed, the story of their meeting and subsequent relationship has since passed into Hollywood mythology, not least because Givenchy received no screen credit for his designs for Hepburn when she appeared in the role of Sabrina Fairchild in the Paramount release *Sabrina*. Instead, the story goes, Paramount costume designer Edith Head, received the screen credit and the Academy Award for Best Costume Design for the film the following year. Despite the lack of acknowledgement for Givenchy's work on the film, the difference between the couturier's styling of Hepburn compared with that of Head was, nonetheless, apparent. In his designs, Givenchy chose to emphasize the star's slender frame, something that Edith Head, had famously attempted to disguise when she had designed the costumes for Hepburn's role in *Roman Holiday* released by Paramount the previous year.

The difference between Hepburn's 'dancer' body and that of other Hollywood stars or 'ordinary' women of the day was noted in fashion magazines, fan magazines and the press of the time; Monahan, writing in 1957, referring to Hepburn as 'ever-so-skinny, but ever-so-talented'. Film director, Billy Wilder was quoted in Lowry as saying, 'This girl may, single-handedly, make the bosom boom a thing of the past.' Hepburn's body type was considered aspirational and, as previously mentioned, carried connotations of European high culture, a point reflected in a press interview, in 1960, with opera singer and actress Anna Maria Alberghetti, quoted by Wilson, who referred to Hepburn as a physical ideal saying, 'I've heard men say, "but she's all bone." That's what I'd like to be, she spells cl-a-s-s.' Nonetheless, Hepburn herself repeatedly made mention of the oddness of her body, particularly her flat chest and large feet, saying, in a quotation used by Wilson, for instance, to one journalist in 1953, 'The trouble is, I don't have pretty feet. They're knobbly.' Ironically, Hepburn's body shape was also cited as the reason for the failure of the Gap skinny black pants campaign. Although the campaign reintroduced Hepburn to the popular consciousness and despite receiving widespread publicity due to the commercial, Hepburn's name did not appear on the Forbes list for 2006. Instead, the *New York Times* declared the television advert a failure, claiming in 2007 that, 'Last fall's commercials for Audrey Hepburn-style skinny black pants turned off women who couldn't imagine their own hindquarters fitting into them.'

Givenchy continued to dress Hepburn both on- and off-screen strengthening an association between the star and the transformative power of couturier fashion, which was reiterated in the narratives of *Sabrina*, *Funny Face* and *My Fair Lady* (George Cukor, 1964). The process of transformation through fashion and expert styling is familiar to audiences of contemporary makeover television shows. For instance, the 'Next Top Model' series, a franchise that began with *America's Next Top Model* (Banks, UPN/ The CW, 2003-) and which has been marketed internationally, includes a 'makeover' episode that is eagerly anticipated by regular viewers due to its focus on the aspiring models who are either resistant to or upset by the changes made to their appearance. The narrative arc of the transformation process echoes that of *Funny Face* in which Hepburn's character is, at first, resistant to the makeover demanded by Maggie Prescott, the editor of the women's magazine, 'Quality', then accepts the changes as a means to an end (a visit to Paris), eventually embracing the transformation that is vital to her ultimate goal, albeit one she is unaware of for most of the film; namely, falling in love with the photographer, Dick Avery (played by Fred Astaire), who 'discovers her'. Only by completing her transformation from dowdy intellectual to fashionable 'Quality' woman can Hepburn's character, Jo Stockton, find love. The entwining of couturier style and passion is expressed in the duet, ''S Wonderful', between Astaire and Hepburn at the end of the film when she sings 'You've made my life so glamorous / You can't blame me for feeling amorous.'

Suitably garbed in a wedding dress, Hepburn's character in *Funny Face* eventually fulfils the heteronormative ideals of a Hollywood makeover, changing from the drab single girl to a glamorous woman in love. A similar transformation happens to Hepburn's character, Eliza Doolittle, in *My Fair Lady*, an adaptation of George Bernard Shaw's stage play, *Pygmalion* (1912). In *My Fair Lady*, Eliza, a flower seller, is taken out of the London slums by Professor Henry Higgins who brags confidently to his friend, Colonel Pickering, that in six months he can 'pass her off as a duchess at an Embassy Ball'. Higgins, a phonetics expert, proceeds to transform Eliza from a 'draggle-tailed guttersnipe' to a duchess, teaching her to speak and behave according to the norms of genteel society. Despite Eliza's sudden ability to speak 'properly', a moment in the film punctuated by the song 'The Rain in Spain' and Higgins's declaration, 'by George, I think she's got it,' Eliza's transformation

Transformation, Fashion and Funny Face
Claire Molloy

Fig. 6: Whitney Houston
recreates the Parisian cafe
dance scene in the video for
'I'm Your Baby Tonight'.

is made apparent through the costume design, which, parallels her process of refinement by assuming a more elegant, even demure, quality, as the film progresses.

Her entrance to civil society is marked by a spectacular long-shot of Eliza in a black-and-white costume designed by Cecil Beaton, arriving at the Ascot races. However, Eliza has not achieved a full transformation at this point in the film and the figure-hugging floor-length gown, enormous wide-brimmed hat, overly fussy parasol and bag echoes this; the image is flamboyant, the over-adornment almost vulgar, hinting to Eliza's uncouth background. At the races there is a slippage between duchess and guttersnipe that is revealed when, caught-up in the excitement of a race, Eliza relapses back to her previous vocabulary, screaming 'Come on Dover. Move your bloomin' arse.' The ostentatiousness of the Ascot gown is later replaced by the simplified elegance of Hepburn's costume for the Embassy Ball, the refinement of the dress reflecting the eventual cultivation of Eliza, who is now ready to pass as a duchess. Eliza, similar to Hepburn's role as Jo in *Funny Face*, falls in love with the man responsible for initiating her makeover, finally being worthy of his love when she eventually embraces her new self-image.

So many references to Hepburn and her films are invested with the idea of an almost magical transformation. In a *Will and Grace* storyline about a 'gay makeover', where Will and Jack transform Karen Walker's cousin into a 'proper' gay man, the series references *My Fair Lady* in a narrative arc that spans four episodes entitled 'Fagmalion Part One: Gay it Forward', (Season 5, episode 13) 'Fagmalion Part Two: Attack of the Clones' (Season 5, episode 14), 'Fagmalion Part Three: Bye Bye Beardy' (Season 5, episode 17) and 'Fagmalion Part Four: The Guy Who Loved Me' (season 5, episode 18). In the Gap skinny pant advert, CGI technology is used to transform Hepburn from the free-thinking idealist in *Funny Face* to the cartoon-like character who cavorts around the khaki-coloured kaleidoscopic world of contemporary high-street fashion before being deposited back into the basement cafe of the original film footage. In the video for 'Countdown', Beyoncé moves from one world to another, transforming herself into other iconic women of popular culture – Diana Ross, Twiggy, Bardot and Hepburn in *Funny Face* – a process of postmodern mimicry that harkens back to Madonna's transformations from one movie star to another in the music video for 'Vogue' (1990).

Released six months after 'Vogue', the video for 'I'm Your Baby Tonight', also adopts a loose narrative of transformation, with Houston walking through a mirror, Alice-like, to transform into Dietrich, Diana Ross and, of course, Audrey Hepburn, complete with black turtleneck, black skinny pants and ballet pumps performing in a recreation of the bohemian Paris cafe. In reusing Hepburn's image, we are reminded of the potency of stories of transformation and the desires of a 'makeover' culture. ●

GO FURTHER

Books

Growing Up With Audrey Hepburn: Text, Audience, Resonance
Rachael Moseley
(Manchester: MUP, 2002)
Dyer, Richard (1985) 'Entertainment and Utopia' in Nichols, Bill (ed) (1985) *Movies and Methods Vol. II*. Berkley and Los Angeles: California University Press, pp.220-232.

Streitmatter, Rodger (2009) *From "Perverts" to "Fab Five": The Media's Changing Depiction of Gay Men and Lesbians*. New York & London: Routledge.

Extracts/Essays/Articles

Lowry, Cynthia (1954) 'Audrey Hepburn sets style for 1954 beauty'
in *The Leader-Post*, 26 March 1954 p.6.
Milwaukee Journal, 'Reviewing the Screen' 3 May 1957, Part 2, p.11.

Monahan, Kaspar (1957) ''Funny Face' a Delight', *The Pittsburgh Press*, 19 April 1957, p.12.

Wilson, Earl (1953) 'Audrey Hepburn's Exotic in a Checked Tablecloth'
in *The Milwaukee Sentinel*, 25 August 1953, p.9.

Wilson, Earl (1960) 'Anna Maria Loses Weight; New Boyfriend on Hand'
in *The Toledo Blade*, 12 November 1960, p.12.

Online

Atkinson, Clare (2007) 'Gap Tries Somewhat Of An Old-Fashioned Campaign', 3 August 2007, online at http://www.nytimes.com/2007/08/03/business/media/03adco.html [accessed 18 August 2012].

Keehner, Jonathan & Coleman-Lochner, Lauren (2011) 'Dead-Celebrity Dealmaker Salter Buys Marilyn Monroe Name', 13 January 2011, online at http://www.bloomberg.com/news/2011-01-13/dead-celebrity-dealmaker-salter-buys-marilyn-monroe-name.html [accessed 18 August 2012].

Transformation, Fashion and Funny Face
Claire Molloy

Miller, Daniel (2006) 'Audrey Hepburn: Dead is the new alive' 15 September 2006, online at http://www.huffingtonpost.com/danny-miller/audrey-hepburn-dead-is-th_b_29484.html [accessed 18 August 2012].

NBCNews.com (2006) 'Test Pattern: Hepburn Falls into the Gap' 6 October 2006 online at http://today.msnbc.msn.com/id/14854161/ns/today-entertainment/t/test-pattern-hepburn-falls-gap/ [Accessed 18 August 2012].

Television

'The Buying Game' *Will and Grace*, Season 1, episode 8
'Fagmalion Part One: Gay it Forward', *Will and Grace*, Season 5, episode 13
'Fagmalion Part Two: Attack of the Clones', *Will and Grace*, Season 5, episode 14
'Fagmalion Part Three: Bye Bye Beardy', *Will and Grace*, Season 5, episode 17
'Fagmalion Part Four: The Guy Who Loved Me', *Will and Grace*, Season 5, episode 18

‘CLOTHES, *PER SE*,
THE COSTUME IS TERRIBLY
IMPORTANT TO ME,
ALWAYS HAS BEEN.
PERHAPS BECAUSE I DIDN'T
HAVE ANY TECHNIQUE FOR
ACTING WHEN I STARTED
BECAUSE I HAD NEVER
LEARNED TO ACT.
I HAD A SORT OF
MAKE-BELIEVE,
LIKE CHILDREN DO'.

AUDREY HEPBURN

Chapter
5

Audrey Hepburn and the Popularization of the 'Little Black Dress'

Andrew Howe

→ In 1961, French designer Hubert de Givenchy designed a black sheath dress to be worn by Audrey Hepburn in the film *Breakfast at Tiffany's* (Blake Edwards, 1961). By this time, Hepburn's acting career was in a minor slump. After breaking into Hollywood as the post-war 'It Girl' with *Roman Holiday* (William Wyler, 1953), Hepburn had starred in a series of films that were both popularly and critically acclaimed, including *Sabrina* (Billy Wilder, 1954), *Funny Face* (Stanley Donen, 1957), and *Love in the Afternoon* (Billy Wilder, 1957).

Fig. 1: Hepburn in the little black dress.

However, by the end of the decade several poorly received films, compounded by personal problems including two miscarriages, resulted in what looked to be a decline for the star both personally and professionally. This all changed in 1960, however, when Hepburn returned to film-making after recovering from a broken back and having given birth to a son. Cast by Blake Edwards for the film adaptation of Truman Capote's 1958 novella of the same name, Hepburn turned to longtime friend and fashion collaborator Givenchy in order to design a dress (Figure 1) for the opening scene ('Hubert de Givenchy'). The fashion designer sought for simplicity in designing an outfit for a character from humble beginnings but who held grandiose dreams. What resulted was the rarest combination between model and wardrobe, as flesh and cloth conspired to create an iconic image that, over fifty years later, still enjoys a high degree of cultural currency. This chapter explores what became known as the 'little black dress', an ensemble that is arguably Audrey Hepburn's largest contribution to the field of fashion.

A history of the little black dress
Although it did not carry the name 'little black dress' until the 1960s, and simple black dresses had been around a long time before Hepburn starred in *Breakfast at Tiffany's*, as

Audrey Hepburn and the Popularization of the 'Little Black Dress'
Andrew Howe

Fig. 2: Coco Chanel's 1926 concept sketch.

noted by Maura Fritz, the design first rose to the level of cultural consciousness during the 1920s. Known as the 'Roaring Twenties', this decade marked a period of relative economic wealth throughout the United States. Danelle Moon notes that it was marked by a period of post-war optimism as well as sexual liberation (pp. 85–86). Veterans returning to the United States brought with them new ideas about sexuality, many of which were influenced by more continental European views. Dances such as the Charleston become popular during this time period and were noteworthy for allowing women greater bodily expression. Despite its illegality due to the Volstead Act (1919), the consumption of alcohol was commonplace during this time, including among women who, for the first time, were accompanying men to clubs and public music halls (see 'Raise a glass to Prohibition'). Nowhere were changes in gender more evident, however, than in the field of fashion, where new markers of beauty anticipated, among other things, the look that Hepburn would later cultivate. The style that began to emerge among the young women of the Roaring Twenties was one of relative androgyny, with breasts generally bound flat and hair cut into a bob, often hidden under a hat. And to top it all off, the dress of choice was black and form-fitting, showcasing the legs but also serving to reduce the bust, thus highlighting more androgynous features.

These new trends in fashion generally fit into the era's wider narrative of freedom from restrictive gender roles that also implicated the ability for the new woman to dance, drink and listen to music along with the men. These women were known as Flappers and, as is often the case, actresses in Hollywood led the way in establishing this new look. Although it is difficult to know for sure which fashion designer popularized this style of dress – a sketch of Coco Chanel's featuring a simple black dress (Figure 2) dates back to 1926 (see 'A Short History of the Little Black Dress'), but such dresses had already begun to appear – the same cannot be said of Hollywood.

Louise Brooks was a popular movie star and Flapper, as was Clara Bow, the first of a long line of Hollywood starlets to be designated the 'It Girl', a list that would eventually include Audrey Hepburn. Brooks and Bow helped to popularize the little black dress, but the Flapper who made this look famous was ironically not an actor but instead a cartoon character. Created by Max Fleischer in 1930, Betty Boop danced her way into the hearts of an American population beginning to come to grips with the realities of the Great Depression. Although not appearing until after the Roaring Twenties had come to a conclusion, Betty Boop captured the zeitgeist of the times. Her fashion sense, playful sexuality and propensity for misadventure resonated with the public and separated her from more childish and sanitized female cartoon characters such as Minnie Mouse. Much like Audrey Hepburn would a generation later, Betty Boop maintained a semblance of innocence despite her overt sexuality, allowing her to appeal to a much larger audience. Although she was more full-figured than had been the norm during the Flapper era, Betty Boop extended this era's fashion sensibilities and became associated with the little black dress (Figure 3). She would appear in many other outfits during the cartoon's run,

Fig. 3: Betty Boop, Flapper and predecessor to Hepburn.

Fig. 4: World War II's Rosie the Riveter and the move toward practical fashion

but her black dress would in essence become a de facto uniform.

Despite Betty Boop's popularity, the little black dress declined as a fashion staple during the 1930s. It is no surprise that gendered anxieties were rampant within a male population that was largely out of work. Among other cultural pressures, the threat to masculinity posed by unemployment led to a renewed conservatism within gender roles, which served to impact fashion in similarly conservative ways (Lauren Olds). The 1940s saw the widespread entrance of women into the workforce, as most of the able-bodied men were overseas fighting World War II. As noted on *The People History.com*, this transition from domestic space to workplace resulted in a certain practicality of fashion. For instance, silk blouses were replaced by denim shirts, as silk was needed for parachutes and other wartime supplies and denim was better suited for withstanding the rigours of factory life. Propaganda posters such as the famed one featuring Rosie the Riveter (Figure 4) indicated how work impacted fashion during this time period (see 'World War Women – Rosie the Riveter'). Following the war, the returning soldiers needed jobs and women were expected to leave the factories. Once again, the fashion of the time reflected such cultural imperatives, and a more feminine style quickly evolved. As noted by the Metropolitan Museum of Art, Christian Dior's 1947 'New Look' line featured a cinched waist, accentuated bosom and hips, and prominent shoulders. Edwardian ideals of feminine beauty once again reigned, with glamorous and full-figured women such as Jane Russell and Marilyn Monroe the primary fashion icons. The little black dress, as well as its stylistic minimalism, had long been forgotten.

Hepburn, Givenchy and *Breakfast at Tiffany's*

It was into this world that Hepburn and Givenchy entered, forever changing the landscape of fashion by introducing a look predicated upon simplicity and designed for a much thinner model. In the look that she cultivated, Audrey Hepburn was a throwback to the Flappers, although the roles for which her character had a bobbed haircut (*Roman Holiday* and *Funny Face*) were not the ones where she popularized the Flapper-inspired dress. Although Givenchy and Hepburn had collaborated ever since *Sabrina*, a film for which he designed a less well-known little black dress for her to wear, their partnership entered new territory with *Breakfast at Tiffany's* (Figure 5). This film's popularity was so widespread that its most famous article of clothing inspired numerous imitators. Some designers merely copied Givenchy, whereas others began to push the envelope in how much complexity they could bring to what was a fundamentally simple motif. Despite the limitations of colour imposed upon this design, there were a number of different materials and design features that gave designers a never-ending supply of possible iterations. The dress could be with or without straps and sleeves, and extend to the thigh, knee, calf or feet. It could either accentuate or downplay the bosom, and employ a plunging neckline or be cut straight across. Different materials could provide the base, such as satin or leather, and sequins and other materials could be used for

Audrey Hepburn and the Popularization of the 'Little Black Dress'
Andrew Howe

Fig. 5: Givenchy at work.

adornment. The dress used in *Breakfast at Tiffany's*, however, was so monumental in its influence that the little black dress has been relatively conservative ever since. Indeed, most modern iterations are only slightly embellished, perhaps due to the fact that Hepburn over-accessorized with a tiara, pearls, opera gloves and an ostentatious, foot-long cigarette holder (Figure 6). Apparently, the only way to distinguish oneself from the progenitor who wore *the* little black dress is to under-accessorize. As fashion designer Karl Lagerfeld once noted, it is exactly this simplicity that has allowed the dress to have such a timeless look:

Since it was invented there has always been a little black dress in the spirit of the moment. Women are never over- or underdressed with a little black dress. A woman never looks bad in one; she can always trust that look. (see *The Classic Woman.me*)

Fig. 6: Iconic film poster featuring dress and ensemble.

The iconic image from *Breakfast at Tiffany's* still enjoys tremendous cultural penetration in contemporary times, and can be found on posters, puzzles, T-shirts, mugs, and many other items throughout the full sweep of popular culture. Aside from a very simple and pleasing look, the ensemble worked on a narrative level within a film that would achieve tremendous and enduring popularity. The film centres upon Paul Varjak (George Peppard), who lives in the same apartment building as Holly Golightly (Audrey Hepburn). The two begin to slowly fall in love with one another, although both are involved in other romantic entanglements and various miscellaneous issues conspire to keep them apart. Holly is a free spirit who dates wealthy men, and it is not until he has known her for a while that Paul finds out about her troubled background. She was born Lula Mae Barnes in rural Texas and was married to a much older man when she was only 14 years old, running away to New York City when she had a chance. The little black dress and its ensemble represent the life to which Holly aspires – Madison Avenue, nights at the opera and, quintessentially, breakfast at Tiffany's. This desire for high society is manifest in the film's opening scene, where a cab delivers Holly to Tiffany & Co. so that she can window-shop while eating a pastry (Figure 7). This scene establishes the tension that will predominate throughout the film, one of dreams and aspirations and the sacrifices, sometimes unacceptable, necessary to achieve them. The dress she wears in this scene lies at the emotional core of this tension. Obviously, due to the formality of her attire, Holly has spent the night moving within the social circles she aspires to inhabit on a more permanent basis. The dark glasses, which are absent in the iconic promotional poster for the film, are evidence of the long hours she has put toward her goal. However, the title of the film is ironic in that Tiffany's does not serve breakfast, and Holly's window shopping suggests that she may not be given a diamond ring, or alternately that her goals in this regard might change. Her attire may be the closest that she will ever get to high society, as in a cursory way it does mark her as belonging. The dress is an object that can be taken off just as easily as it is put on, symbolizing the manner in which Holly

Fig. 7: Hepburn as Holly Golightly window shopping in front of Tiffany & Co.

shuttles between the worlds of reality and illusion, actuality and aspiration.

Ultimately, you cannot take the rural south out of the girl, and Holly's appearance in the little black dress is counterpointed when she unwinds in her own apartment, most notably in the scene where she sings 'Moon River' on the fire escape while wearing jeans, an unadorned long-sleeved shirt, and her hair pulled up in a scarf. The tension between origins and aspirations is linked not only to physical geography (rural Texas vs. urban New York City) but also to her sartorial choices. With her high-class uniform, the pearls denote wealth, the gloves and cigarette holder suggest upper-class leisure activities such as operas and cocktail parties, and the tiara brings to mind the desire for a Cinderella-like fairy tale. Clearly, not all viewers had the same aspirations as the character of Holly Golightly, and not all would have identified with such a material aim in securing a Tiffany's diamond ring from a wealthy suitor. However, the simplicity of the black dress mitigates the ostentatiousness of the rest of the ensemble, making Holly's goals more palatable to the viewer. The film's qualities, including Audrey's character and the way she was dressed symbolically, combined to establish within the general viewership a nostalgic feeling about dreams. Indeed, the film's opening has maintained its potency over the decades, and the filming of this scene was used to frame the 2000 made-for-television biopic *The Audrey Hepburn Story* (Steven Robman). Not all aspects of the film have weathered the test of time, however. Mickey Rooney's 'yellowface' portrayal of Holly's annoying Japanese American neighbour, Mr Yunioshi, has come under scrutiny for its racist qualities, as noted by *Michelle I*. However, the growth of second wave feminism during the 1970s failed to tarnish the image of either Holly Golightly or Audrey Hepburn.

Hepburn's fashion legacy

The popularity of *Breakfast at Tiffany's* reinvigorated Hepburn's career, making her an even bigger fashion icon throughout her thirties than she had been during her twenties. She maintained her relationship with Givenchy, and along with Jacqueline Bouvier Kennedy helped make him one of the most sought after fashion designers in the world. He continued to design dresses for her, both in her cinematic roles and in real life. Several of these were noteworthy in and of themselves, including dresses worn by character Regina Lampert in *Charade* (Stanley Donen, 1963) and by character Eliza Doolittle in

Audrey Hepburn and the Popularization of the 'Little Black Dress'
Andrew Howe

Fig. 8: Hepburn and partner Robert Wolders meeting with President Reagan.

My Fair Lady (George Cukor, 1964). There were multiple black dresses worn in *Charade*, which when matched with an oversized pair of sunglasses in the opening scene referenced *Breakfast at Tiffany's*. Givenchy's impact upon Hepburn's look cannot be understated, but he also owed her a very large debt as well. As noted on the *Clothing and Fashion Encyclopedia* website Givenchy gave Hepburn credit not only for helping him in his career, but also serving as a source of inspiration: 'often ideas would come to me when I had her on my mind.' Of all the famous dresses he designed, including the one worn by Hepburn for her acceptance of the Academy Award for Best Actress (*Roman Holiday*) and the one worn by Jacqueline Kennedy to her husband's funeral, it was the little black dress from *Breakfast at Tiffany's* for which he will be forever remembered. Indeed, Hepburn realized this about her own fashion legacy, choosing to wear simple black dresses on several other occasions, ones marked for their importance. In the late 1960s, Hepburn decided to stop acting on a regular basis and spend more time with her family. She became increasingly involved with humanitarian projects, most famously with UNICEF. She was celebrated for her humanitarian work by two presidents, and when invited to the White House by President Ronald Reagan in 1981 wore a simple but elegant black dress (see 'Meeting with Celebrities') (Figure 8).

Having helped popularize this dress twenty years earlier, she now wore it during a time when new fashion designers were rising to prominence. Several of the most notable designers and stars would team up in the 1990s with the little black dress, including Princess Diana, who famously stepped out in a Christina Stambolian dress in 1994, as shown on *Xfinity.com* (Figure 9). Two celebrities in the post-millenial period, however, have taken the dress to new heights. Linked together in the popular imagination due to their romantic ties to Brad Pitt and their propensity for showing up in the tabloids, Jennifer Aniston and Angelina Jolie have, on many occasions, attended premiers, awards ceremonies and other public functions sporting black dresses. During January 2012, Jolie wore a Jenny Packham full-length sheath dress to the awards show of the Producer's Guild of America (Packham having recently become well known for designing, among other clothing items, simple black dresses for another British princess, Kate Middleton).

Not to be outdone, the next week, as reported by the *Daily Mail*, Aniston wore a beaded, form-fitting mid-thigh dress to the awards show of the Director's Guild of America. Clearly, both starlets were taking a page from Hepburn, realizing that black is universal across generations and that a lack of ornamentation would help establish a timeless look. These icons of the modern era have made their most significant fashion statements by following in the footsteps of Audrey Hepburn.

Although Hepburn herself did not innovate the little black dress, and others have worn it to great attention and acclaim, her version will always endure. Indeed, in 2006, fully 45 years after the dress from *Breakfast at Tiffany's* entered into the collective con-

Fig. 9: Diana, Princess of Wales in a little black dress.

sciousness, one of the three Givenchy created for the film sold at a Christie's auction for over £460,000 (see 'Sale 4912/Lot 111'). That same year, the clothing store Gap (known colloquially as 'The Gap') capitalized upon the success of Hepburn's association with the little black dress with their sale of the 'skinny black pant' (Figure 10).

Showing footage of Hepburn dancing from Funny Face and set to the AC/DC song 'Back in Black', The Gap kicked off their very successful 'Keep it Simple'(2006) campaign, which pushed form-fitting black slacks and other articles of casual simplicity. The tagline, 'It's Back, the Skinny Black Pant', coupled with Hepburn as a spokesperson from the past, established The Gap as a company selling a more casual version of the little black dress suited for the modern woman (see the YouTube video 'Audrey Hepburn In Skinny Black Pants'). Although twenty years have passed since her death, Audrey Hepburn can still sell a line of clothing, but her legacy remains the little black dress. It was first noted long before she arrived in Hollywood and has continued to play a huge role in fashion long after she exited stage right, but Audrey Hepburn has become inexorably associated with this fashion piece. Many wore it before her, many after, and some of them famously, but actresses and models and celebrities as diverse as Clara Bow and Princess Diana will never knock Heburn off of this particular pedastel of fashion. As the ultimate demonstration of this fact, Hepburn's name has entered the lexicon of fashion to denote this dress, as a quote by fashion designer Betsy Thompson on *Thinkexist.com* establishes: 'Black is very strong this season, especially black head-to-toe in varying textures. Black outfits are being paired with a single embellishment such as the fabulous little black dress with a pearl detail at the neck – very Audrey Hepburn.' ●

Audrey Hepburn and the Popularization of the 'Little Black Dress'
Andrew Howe

~~~~~~~~~~~~

GO FURTHER

Books

Daily Life of Women During the Civil Rights Era
Danelle Moon
(Santa Barbara: ABC-CLIO, 2011)

Extracts/Essays/Articles

Lauren Olds
'World War II and Fashion: The Birth of the New Look'
In *Constructing the Past*. 2.1 (2001): 47-64.

Online

'A Short History of the Little Black Dress'
Maura Fritz
Real Simple [n.d.], www.realsimple.com/beauty-fashion/clothing/dresses-skirts/little-black-dress-00000000046948/index.html

'Anything You Can Do!'
Daily Mail Reporter
Daily Mail. 30 January 2012, www.dailymail.co.uk/tvshowbiz/article-2093337/

'Audrey Hepburn in Skinny Black Pants' [YouTube], 4 December 2006, www.youtube.com/watch?v=_g_VQJcx-rU

'Betsy Thompson Quotes'. *Thinkexist.com* [n.d.], thinkexist.com/quotes/betsy_thompson/

'Christian Dior (1905–1957)'. *The Metropolitan Museum of Art* [n.d.], www.metmuseum.org/toah/hd/dior/hd_dior.htm/

'Hubert de Givenchy'. *Clothing and Fashion Encyclopedia* [n.d.], angelasancartier.net/hubert-de-givenchy.

'Meeting with Celebrities'. *The Ronald Reagan Presidential Library and Museum* [n.d.], www.reagan.utexas.edu/archives/photographs/celebrities.html

'Pre-War and Post-War 1940s Fashion Trends'. *The People History* [n.d.], www.thepeoplehistory.com/40sclothes.html

'Princess Diana's Style'. *Xfinity* [n.d.], xfinity.comcast.net/slideshow/news-princessdianasstyle/28/

'Raise a glass to Prohibition'. *Yesteryear Essentials* [WordPress] [n.d.], yesteryearessentials.wordpress.com/tag/volstead-act/

'Sale 4912/Lot 111'. *Christie's* [n.d.], www.christies.com/LotFinder/lot_details.aspx?intObjectID=4832498

'World War Women'. *Glamour Daze*, 29 October 2010, glamourdaze.com/2010/10/world-war-two-women-rosie-riveter.html

'Yellow: A Story in Pictures'
Michelle I.
Race Bending. 9 December 2009, www.racebending.com/v3/background/history-of-yellowface/

Chapter
6

'She's Enchanting': How Her Neglected Films Give Fans the Key to Audrey-ness

Jacqui Miller

→ **Just the single word 'Audrey' will conjure in most people's minds a vision that is at once tantalizingly ephemeral and yet composed of quite specific elements: a slim figure, girlish charm, timeless style and a dancer's feline grace. Certain adjectives also recur: Audrey was – and her image is – enchanting (as we see in the above quotation taken from one of her earliest films, *The Secret People*), lovely, charming.**

Trying to pin down the source and perpetuation of this Audrey-ness is part of this book's premise and runs throughout each chapter. As Audrey's main body of work was her films, presumably its starting point at least lies there. Is it so simple? Despite continuing to generate reverence far greater than that afforded to any other star, and having a name that is a synonym amongst film, beauty, fashion and lifestyle fans worldwide, Audrey-ness seems to arise from just a handful of films: *Roman Holiday* (William Wyler, 1953), *Sabrina* (Billy Wilder, 1954), *Funny Face* (Stanley Donen, 1957), *Breakfast at Tiffany's* (Blake Edwards, 1961) and *Charade* (Stanley Donen, 1963), with one or two others, *My Fair Lady* (George Cukor, 1964) and *How to Steal a Million* (William Wyler, 1966) making less notable but honourable contributions. Audrey's career was about much more than these few movies but her filmography includes many which the most Audrey-obsessed style blogger or lifestyle devotee would fail to name, and which are all but unknown today except to film historians. These may include big budget epics such as *War and Peace* (King Vidor, 1956), box office hits of the day such as *The Nun's Story* (Fred Zinnemann, 1959) and off-beat experiments such as *Two for the Road* (Stanley Donen, 1967) as well as films that frankly sank without trace even upon first release, such as *Green Mansions* (Mel Ferrer, 1959) and *The Unforgiven* (John Huston, 1960). However it is my belief that unlocking the key to Audrey-ness lies in bringing the neglected films alongside their celebrated peers. The forgotten films in fact uncannily anticipate the key elements to Audrey's iconography and enable fans to realize they knew the secret to Audrey-ness all along.

The Secret People: 'She's enchanting'

The Secret People (Sidney Cole, 1952), is an Ealing Studios-produced British film which gave Audrey her first starring role and name above the credits. It tells a story of terroristic resistance to an unspecified Balkan dictatorship. Eleanora 'Nora' (Audrey) and her elder sister, Maria (Valentina Cortese) are sent in 1930 from their dangerous homeland to stay with a friend of their father's, the affable London cafe owner, Anselmo (Charles Goldner), although word soon arrives that their father has been killed by the regime because of his pacifistic political ideals. Fast-forward to 1937 and the sisters become naturalized British citizens and are taken on holiday to Paris by Anselmo where they are reunited with Maria's former lover Sergei (Louis Balan) who is now active in the terrorist resistance and, back in London, fatally draws Maria into the group as his pawn. What is important about this early film is that it serves both as a reflection of Audrey's life to this point, and a predictor of her future career and fandom persona.

Part of Audrey's 'class' is her Euro-aristocratic lineage; a Dutch mother, the redoubtable Baroness Ella van Heemstra and a father of less transparent background, the British-passport-holding, Belgian-born (although some sources say Austrian) Joseph Hepburn-Ruston (in fact the 'Hepburn' strand is fallacious – a non-existent association by marriage with the lineage of Mary Queen of Scots). From the outset, this European-

'She's Enchanting': How Her Neglected Films Give Fans the Key to Audrey-ness
Jacqui Miller

Fig. 1: She's enchanting.

Fig. 2: She'll be a hep cat soon.

ness and its associations of mystery are transmitted by *The Secret People* although the sisters' father reverses Hepburn-Ruston's notorious Nazi sympathies which continue to be glossed over by many Audrey style guides. Nora's experience of having to cross Europe to escape dictatorship also reflects Audrey's own childhood as her mother took her from Belgium to England to Holland to try to find a safe berth from the Nazis. Even at this tender age, Audrey exhibited an aura of mystique. A childhood friend quoted in Donald Spoto's biography remembered her leaving their English village for Holland: 'She had come to us unexpectedly – she left us just as mysteriously'; words that are an uncanny parallel with *The Secret People*'s opening title card: 'Hidden in each one of us is a secret person.' Baroness Ella's war-time decision to return with Audrey to her native Holland led to their near-starvation. Subsisting on little more than weeds and scavenged tulip bulbs, Audrey was close to starvation by the war's end, and her eternal slimness is often accounted to damage to her metabolism that this period wrought. Again Nora evokes Audrey when she faints upon arrival at Anselmo's; the doctor prescribes 'a good tonic and plenty of milk' to build her up.

Another integral facet of Audrey-ness is her physical grace, associated with her formative ballet dancing and captured in the title of Robyn Karney's biography *Audrey Hepburn: A Star Danced* (1993). She resolutely pursued her dance training even during the war and sought to make this her career in post-war London. In this, Nora and Audrey's lives are almost interchangeable. Audrey was a driven young woman, perhaps at almost 5 feet 7 inches and not quite talented enough to make it as a prima ballerina, now seeking a career on the London stage and soon in films. Her pursuit of a part in *The Secret People*, besieging the studio to see if it had 'anything in it for me' is an exact match for Nora's quest for a ballet part in a London cabaret; Nora's bedroom walls are bedecked with pictures of dancers taken from magazines in just the way we could imagine Audrey's teenage dreams. The audition is held in a ballet studio rehearsal room and the first on-screen crystallization of Audrey's eternal image comes when the show's benefactress (Athene Seyler) sighs: 'She's enchanting.' This term will always epitomize Audrey, forming the title of Donald Spoto's biography, *Enchantment: The Life of Audrey Hepburn* (2006).

Like Audrey, part of Nora's charm is her free-spirited vivacity and zest for life. This time predicting rather than paralleling Audrey's career, during the holiday in Paris we

see Nora dance for the first time in a nightclub. As we can see in Figure 2, she loses herself in the free and easy atmosphere and is exactly like Jo Stockton cavorting with feline grace amongst the empatheticalists of *Funny Face.*

Later, as Nora's star ascends and she performs at a gala, another element of future Audrey-ness is confirmed (and a prefiguration of a comment made in *My Fair Lady* as Henry Higgins (Rex Harrison) triumphantly presents Eliza (Audrey) at the embassy ball); a member of the audience exactly captures her essence: 'She looks charming.'

War and Peace: Like holding springtime in your arms

Melissa Hellstern, author of one of the best-selling style guides, *How to be Lovely: The Audrey Hepburn Way of Life* (2005), spoke on behalf of all Audrey fans: 'To the world Audrey would forever be a princess.' *Roman Holiday*'s Princess Ann may have begun this process, and is her most remembered regal character, but Audrey played another aristocrat, one that is less well known, but also one that captured a range of Audrey-ness revealing her to be as multifaceted as one of Tiffany's jewels.

In King Vidor's cinemation of *War and Peace* (Leo Tolstoy, 1869), Audrey played Natasha, a part Tolstoy could have written with her in mind: 'A black-eyed, wide-mouthed girl […] at that charming age when a girl is no longer a child, though that child is not yet a young woman.' Critics agreed that she exactly captured Natasha's look, but as a character, she remained too 'Audrey' to be convincing. Leaving aside the quality of her acting, this film certainly marked the point at which Audrey-ness was coming together as a deliberate construction. As Alexander Walker notes, she was bringing together her own 'court circle', the hair and make-up people who would work with her throughout her career, ensuring she would always look 'Audrey'. In fact, the film almost seems to reflect on what defined Audrey's style and differentiated her from the stereotyped, Hollywoodized starlet. Billy Wilder, her director on *Sabrina* and *Love in the Afternoon* (1957) famously declared that Audrey was 'the girl most likely to single-handedly make bosoms a thing of the past', something which Natasha almost muses upon. Her 'love-rival' for Count Pierre (Henry Fonda) is played by bosomy blonde Anita Ekberg who looks every inch the 1950s sex goddess in the model of Monroe or Jayne Mansfield. Natasha observes of Helene, making an implicit reference to Audrey's ushering in a new girlish style which made the sex-bombs almost mumsy: 'I'd like to be like her when I grow up,' before add-

'She's Enchanting': How Her Neglected Films Give Fans the Key to Audrey-ness
Jacqui Miller

Fig. 4: Like holding spring-time in your arms.

ing, with a glance at her girlish chest, 'of course I'd have to fill out around here.'

Natasha does remind the viewer of Princess Ann. When we first meet her she is look-ing out of her palace window longing for adventure, and at the ball where her romance with Prince Andrei takes flight her struggle to maintain formal composure over youthful vitality is captured when she asks her brother if everyone is looking at her. When he asks can't she see for herself, Natasha replies: 'Not without changing expression,' an answer which evokes Princess Ann's struggle to keep her pose greeting guests whilst losing the shoe she has slipped off beneath her ball gown. The delightful sense of a girl on the cusp of womanhood that we have seen in Nora, Princess Ann and Sabrina, as well as Nora's dancing and Audrey's feline grace, is captured in Prince Andrei's love-struck contem-plation of Natasha: 'What a joy it is to dance with her. Like holding springtime in your arms. Like holding a branch of lilac or a kitten.' Natasha also continues to capture Sab-rina's sorceress-like charms; on moonlit nights, she wants to hold herself tight 'and fly off to the moon', casting a spell on Andrei as he overhears her. After her engagement to Andrei is announced, phrases such as: 'how lovely you are' and 'she's enchanting' again anticipate *My Fair Lady* and show that these terms are a de rigueur part of Audrey-ness.

Although *War and Peace* seems to be a meeting place between the early and later 'fairy tale' transformation films, Natasha also has distinct if unexpected affinities with Holly Golightly. As well as Natasha's tiaras and beribboned hats predicting Holly's most famous costumes, the Russian aristocrat and New York good-time girl hold similar views and make similar faux pas in their relationships. Holly has no hypocrisy about sexuality as part of 1960s life, but this is not so different to Natasha's unabashed earthiness; when Nicholas returns from battle and merely shakes Sonia's hand she chides him: 'What's the point in coming home from war if that's all you're going to do'? Holly plays the field while waiting to hook a husband from America's rich list and Natasha too seems to see men as play-things. Pierre suggests love as a pleasure to add to her list, but she is dis-missive, intending to fall in love ten or eleven times, but only for recreation and I'll keep changing partners like a dance. When I finally say I love you to any man and really mean it, it will be like a defeated general surrendering and handing his sword to his enemy.

When both girls find apparent love, their emotional naivety wrecks things; Holly's arrest over her unwitting 'weather reports' to drugs baron Sally Tomato scares away Bra-zilian millionaire, Jose, and Natasha's dalliance with Anatole, ends her engagement to

. *Fig. 5: Rachel – or Holly? –*
stealing turkey eggs.

Andrei. Of course, these being Audrey films, they find true love by the film's close, Natasha with Pierre and Holly with Paul.

The Unforgiven and *Green Mansions*: Holly Golightly's long-lost sisters

John Huston's *The Unforgiven* is one of Audrey's least known films and it is easy to see why. A largely undistinguished western which re-treads ground far more successfully covered by John Ford in (*The Searchers*, 1956) Audrey plays Rachel, a Native American girl who has been adopted as a baby and raised as white by the Zachary family. Although she displays her usual doe-eyed beauty – how could she not – there is little in this film that adds to the mosaic of Audrey-ness, with one exception. Despite Holly Golightly's urbane New York chic, she hails from the South and her clipped accent required much training. For fans, there are really two Holly Golightlys, both of whom represent facets of Audrey-ness. There is the stylish fashionista, but there is also the dressed-down country girl in pedal pushers, a sweater and ballet pumps crooning 'Moon River' to an acoustic guitar on her fire-escape; after all, when Audrey died, Tiffany's tribute to her was the placing of a card reading 'our Huckleberry friend' in their store-windows. Growing up in Texas, her long hair left free, Rachel Zachary exactly anticipates this aspect of Audrey-ness that we might believe originated with Holly. Romping with the animals on the farm, it is as if Rachel is the young Holly in the direct prequel to *Tiffany's*.

In fact these style seeds had already been sown in another film that has dropped almost out of the Audrey canon; *Green Mansions*. Probably more critically derided than any of her other work, in *Green Mansions*, Audrey stars as Rima, a human girl with wood-spirit connotations (when she dies in a forest fire, she is re-incarnated by means of a mythical flower whose characteristics she shares). Living in a South American enchanted forest with a man she believes to be her grandfather (Lee J. Cobb) Rima falls in love with Abel (Tony Perkins) who comes in search of gold to fund his crusade in revolutionary Caracas. As Rima has only one costume throughout, Hubert de Givenchy's services were not used, but this single outfit – a frayed, diaphanous shift – is nonetheless extremely flattering. Clinging, sheer and bias-cut, it skims Audrey's frame to perfection, both embracing her enviable slimness while hinting at provocative curves. Audrey played Holly as a 'kook', a free-wheeling early-1960s beat-girl, who was motivated by the new freedoms of the early 1960s and in this, we could imagine Holly, as the decade unfolded, joining the revellers at Woodstock or the Isle of White. Going barefoot throughout, her lush chestnut hair either worn loose down her back or in bunches or a side-swept ponytail, Rima's look again prefigures aspects of Holly's Audrey-ness. In his biography, Donald Spoto said rather unkindly: 'the entire effect was that of a flower

'She's Enchanting': How Her Neglected Films Give Fans the Key to Audrey-ness
Jacqui Miller

Fig. 6: Kooky Holly's flower-
child sister, Rima.

child from Haight Ashbury.' Rima is also given to musings that could have come from
Hair (Milos Forman, 1979) 'I believe in everything. Every leaf, every flower. Birds. The air
…', and in the 'The Ballad of Green Mansions' Abel calls her 'a child of the moon'. But this
fresh break from old-style glamour and embracement of the new decade is part of what
keeps Audrey at the forefront of twenty-first-century style. The clothes worn by Rachel
Zachary or Rima could equally well be worn by a woman at today's Glastonbury festival
and *Green Mansion*'s continued, if usually unsung, contribution to Audrey-ness is noted
by a post on the blog *no.48* in September 2008: 'It may have been a box office failure but
girl of the rain forest Rima's style did not miss the mark in *Green Mansions*.'

Two for the Road: 'Who are you'? 'Some girl.'
If Audrey is a multifaceted gem, this is most clearly seen in by far the best of her 'unsung' films. Speaking on behalf of Audrey fans, Pamela Keogh's *What Would Audrey Do?
Timeless Lessons for Living with Grace and Style* (2008) describes *Two for the Road*
as 'our favourite movie'. Directed by Stanley Donen, it takes the experimental hints of
Funny Face to new heights, using not only a fractured narrative, but also fast motion,
visual puns and the intercutting of time and space with aplomb. Audrey plays Joanna
and the film's three time-frames trace her meeting and subsequent marriage to Mark
Wallace (Albert Finney).

Audrey style has three key phases, the first two being the gamine and the chic city
fashionista. The gamine, such as Sabrina or Jo Stockton, will become fashionistas, but
so too, the ultimate city-girl, Holly Golightly contained within her the guitar-strumming
gamine who sometimes came out to play on the fire-escape. As the 1960s unfolded,
Audrey's and Holly's rather formal 'little black dress' code morphed into a more free-
wheeling 'mod' style seen in the well-known *Charade* and *How to Steal a Million*. In both
of these films, Audrey was costumed to perfection by Givenchy, but what for fans has
always been one essence of Audrey-ness, the sense that they can access her look, was
brilliantly achieved in *Two for the Road* by Donen's decision that instead of Givenchy,
Joanna should be dressed in the Swinging Sixties designers including King's Road's Mary
Quant and the space-age Paco Rabanne. When Joanna and Mark first meet, on a cross-
Channel ferry, and fall in love hitching across France, she is a gamine. In a red sweater,
jeans and plimsolls, her long hair swept back in a hair-band, she could be a modern day
Rachel Zachary. In their early, happy marriage, she is in controlled fashionista mode;
bubble-cut hair and a Holly-esque trench coat. In *Two for the Road*'s third time-frame,
the troubled marriage years, the wardrobe is mod, mad-cap and edgy, truly capturing
the times including a Paco Rabanne silver dress ('loved' by 72 fans on *AnOthermag.com*)

Fig. 7: 'Quelle gala' as grown-up Holly might have said.

Fig. 7: 'Quelle gala' as grown-up Holly might have said.

Fig. 8: Jo Stockton all grown up.

and a black wet-look patent leather trouser suit. Yet each moment in Joanna's life contains each other, and there are sly hints throughout the film at the icons that construct Audrey-ness. When they first meet, Mark imitates Bogey, the actor who plays gamine Sabrina's beau. In stage two, the early marriage, at a ball, Joanna wears a Holly-style tiara, and murmurs 'quelle gala'. In the final stage, the wet-look trouser-suited Joanna is a latter day Jo Stockton, both in France, both in stylish black.

Two for the Road deconstructs and in so doing demonstrates the construction of Audrey-ness; through her films, her styles, her life. The fact that the film uses time as a rewinding trick; in some scenes we are not quite sure where or when we are, shows how Audrey-ness is always shifting, never fixed, gains additional meaning as time passes, and that early images are re-interpreted in the light of later ones. ●

'She's Enchanting': How Her Neglected Films Give Fans the Key to Audrey-ness
Jacqui Miller

GO FURTHER

Books

What Would Audrey Do? Timeless Lessons for Living with Grace and Style
Pamela Clark Keogh
(London: Aurum, 2008)

Enchantment: The Life of Audrey Hepburn
Donald Spoto
(London: Hutchinson, 2006)

How to be Lovely: The Audrey Hepburn Way of Life
Melissa Hellstern
(London: Robeson, 2005)

Audrey: Her Real Story
Alexander Walker
(London: Orion, 1995)

Audrey Hepburn: A Star Danced
Robyn Karney
(London: Bloomsbury, 1993)

Online

'Style Inspiration: Audrey Hepburn in Green Mansions.' *No. 48* [Blogspot], 29 September
2008, http://no48.blogspot.co.uk/2008_09_01_archive.html.

AnOther, http://www.anothermag.com/

'PICK A DAY. ENJOY IT –
TO THE HILT.
THE DAY AS IT COMES.
PEOPLE AS THEY COME
… THE PAST, I THINK HAS
HELPED ME APPRECIATE
THE PRESENT –
AND I DON'T WANT TO SPOIL
ANY OF IT BY FRETTING
ABOUT THE FUTURE'.

AUDREY HEPBURN

Chapter
7

The Making of an International Star: The Early Film Career and Star Image of Audrey Hepburn, 1948–54

Peter Krämer

→ In this chapter I examine Audrey Hepburn's emergence as one of the twentieth century's most famous international film stars. I concentrate on the years 1948–54, starting with Hepburn's first ever film appearance in an Anglo-Dutch production from 1948 and ending with the year in which she won the Best Actress Oscar for her Hollywood debut *Roman Holiday* (William Wyler, 1953), while the success of her second Hollywood feature *Sabrina* (Billy Wilder, 1954) during the same year confirmed her status as an international superstar.

I first explore the phenomenon of stardom in general terms, before then moving on to the efforts various people made to promote Hepburn to stardom in the late 1940s and early 1950s.

A star can be defined as a performer whose physical presence, skills and personality become the focus of public attention because they are perceived as outstanding and unique. The star's *image* combines her professional performance and characterization with her 'real' personality. The public's curiosity about the latter is fed by press publicity purporting to give insights into the star's private life. The star is on display in professional performances (on stage or screen), usually adopting a fictional *persona* which is assumed to reveal aspects of her 'real' personality. For the privilege of attending these performances, the public is willing to pay. Promoters (agents, casting directors or producers) seek to identify those performers who attract public attention, and to present them to the public. If the promotion is successful, the star becomes a valuable property which can be sold directly to the public or loaned to other producers.

Hepburn's early film career can be seen, then, as a series of three 'discoveries' and promotions, first in the Netherlands in 1947–48, then in England in 1950–51, and finally in the United States between 1951 and 1954. In each instance, there was a close connection between the publicity about her person, and the roles and stories she appeared in. Whether by accident or by design, her public life and her films often fed into each other. Her status changed dramatically in the three promotions: while initially presented as an amateur in the Netherlands, films and publicity during her British period displayed her as a self-consciously sexy starlet, before she was then turned by Hollywood into a fairy-tale film star. All three promotions had an international dimension. In the same way that Hepburn moved easily from one country to another, her promoters operated across national boundaries. Rather than discarding national identity, Hepburn's star image was characterized by multiple national associations, which were the cornerstone of her international marketability. Let's look at each of these promotions in turn.

The first promotion: The Dutch girl in the street

Audrey Hepburn, born Edda Kathleen Hepburn van Heemstra in 1929 in Brussels to an Anglo-Irish father and a Dutch mother, raised in Belgium, England and the Netherlands, was first discovered, at age 18, in Amsterdam, where she attended ballet school and worked as a model. The film-makers Henry Josephson and Charles Van der Linden chose the *amateur* actress for a small role in their feature-length travelogue *Nederlands in Zeven Lessen/Dutch in Seven Lessons*, which premiered on 7 May 1948. The film featured Dutch comedian Wam Heskes as a cameraman and director for the British Rank organization, who comes to Amsterdam to make a documentary about the country in seven days.

The film was financed by Rank, which in its bid for equal status with the major Hollywood studios in the international film market, had set up a worldwide distribution

The Making of an International Star:
The Early Film Career and Star Image of Audrey Hepburn, 1948–54
Peter Krämer

network and theatre chain, including a dozen movie theatres in the Netherlands. When the Dutch government restricted capital exports, Rank was forced to invest some of its Dutch revenues locally. *Dutch in Seven Lessons* was the result of one such investment. Rank also produced a shorter and simplified English-language version entitled *Dutch at the Double*, which could be used as a second feature on double bills in Rank cinemas in the United Kingdom and elsewhere. This version focused on Hepburn, who had only had a minor part in the original.

Hepburn attracts the attention of the British film-maker when he first looks out of his hotel window shortly after his arrival. The audience is invited to see Hepburn as a 'real' KLM stewardess whose willingness to be nice to George and to help him, is an extension of her job. However, another familiar scenario is at work here: the film-maker approaches the young woman with the promise to put her into his film, and she is willing to do whatever is necessary to get her chance of being a film actress. The film-maker keeps his end of the bargain and turns the young woman into the 'star' of his film.

What purports to be a documentary about Holland thus turns into an extended screen test for a performer whose charm and beauty and erotic promise are there for the film-maker and audiences to contemplate. The film's story was mirrored by Charles Van der Linden's professional interest in Hepburn. He took her under contract and sought to create a more conventional narrative vehicle for his discovery, yet failed to get funding.

The second promotion: The British starlet
Rank and the Associated British combine, which between them controlled the British film industry, made a concerted effort after World War II to establish new stars who appealed not only to domestic audiences but could also make British films more marketable abroad, especially in the United States. Rank's 'Charm School', a London based academy for the training and promotion of starlets, which opened in 1946, grew out of this effort. Surprisingly, it took no notice of Hepburn's debut in a Rank production. Instead Hepburn's second discovery took place at Associated British's main studio complex at Elstree, which reopened in 1947–48 and became the basis for extensive campaigns promoting new talents such as Michael Dennison and Richard Todd.

In 1948 Hepburn moved to London where she continued her ballet training and modelling, also taking up acting lessons and appearing in various West End musical revues between December 1948 and July 1950, when she attracted the attention of Elstree's casting director Robert Lennard. In the second half of 1950, she signed a seven-year contract with Associated British and had four tiny parts in comedies made at Elstree and by other studios to which she was loaned. She also became the object of a major publicity campaign. A 1950 press release announced that 'her undoubted talent, her gamin quality of good looks will inject new life into films', mentioning her stage experience both in ballet and in musical revue. Already on 1 April 1951 (when only one of the films,

Fig. 1: *Laughter in Paradise.*

Fig. 2: *The Lavender Hill Mob.*

in which she received a credit, had been released, totalling 45 seconds of screen time), the *Sunday Chronicle* declared her to be 'the most sought after young actress in British films'.

At this point, her appeal was seen to be primarily erotic, an impression which was supported by constant references to the musical revues she had appeared in. On 10 March 1951, the *Evening News*, for example, wrote that 'dancing in a satirical manner with much seductive eye-fluttering is Audrey's speciality on stage' and now on the screen. By this time, her relationship with James Hanson, heir to an extensive family business, was covered by the press, further enhancing the impression that in stereotypical starlet manner Hepburn put her sex appeal to good use. This is precisely what she attempts to do in her first credited film role in Mario Zampi's *Laughter in Paradise* (released in March 1951). Simon and Deniston Russell (played by Guy Middleton and Alastair Sim) have just learned about the difficult tasks set for them in the will of a relative. In order to get his share of the inheritance, Simon, the philandering playboy, is to marry the first woman he talks to. As if she knew about it, Hepburn's cigarette girl seductively approaches the potential heir (see Figure 1).

However, the cigarette girl qualifies merely as a sexual adventure and not as a potential wife. When Simon believes he has found a more appropriate woman, he brings her to the very same restaurant, where the advances of the cigarette girl now have to be rudely rejected. These two scenes are all we see of Hepburn in this film. Hepburn's gold-digger has more luck in Charles Crichton's *The Lavender Hill Mob* (released in June 1951). Henry Holland (played by Alec Guinness), the London clerk who pulled off a robbery and settled with the takings in Rio de Janeiro, has spent his money freely, and acquired an attractive companion in the process, who is a symbol of the good life that money can buy. Hepburn appears only in one brief scene at the beginning where we see her bend fondly over Henry as he gives her a goodbye present of a handful of banknotes (see Figure 2).

To avoid trapping Hepburn in the role of the gold-digging starlet, her promotion had to shift emphasis. In March 1951 she started work on Sidney Cole's *The Secret People*, her first dramatic film, in which she had the substantial role of a ballerina taking refuge from the tyranny of her native Southern European country in London (see Figure 3).

In June she went to Monte Carlo where she played a film star in the French and English versions of a musical comedy entitled *Nous Irons a Monte Carlo/Monte Carlo Baby* (Jean Boyer and Lester Fuller, 1952). The accompanying publicity emphasized her clas-

The Making of an International Star:
The Early Film Career and Star Image of Audrey Hepburn, 1948–54
Peter Krämer

sical ballet training and the fact that she was multilingual. These probably were important factors in her discovery by the French writer Colette in Monte Carlo. Colette chose her to play the title role in Anita Loos's adaptation of her novel *Gigi* (1944), which was to be staged by a French-speaking director, Raymond Rouleau, on Broadway. Hepburn also had a screen test in London and was chosen by William Wyler for the leading role in Paramount's *Roman Holiday* – a central European princess on a goodwill tour to Western Europe escaping her duties for a day in Rome.

Gigi, which opened on Broadway on 24 November 1951 to rave reviews for Hepburn, tells the story of a young girl trained to be a courtesan who gets happily married instead. This mirrored the development of Hepburn, the former starlet, into a serious stage actress, who Paramount, having loaned Hepburn from Associated British, promoted in an international campaign; her marriage with Hanson was imminent following their engagement on 4 December 1951. Hepburn's transformation was summed up in an article in the *Daily Mirror* of 23 January 1952: so far, 'all she had to do was to put over her saucy schoolgirl brand of beauty and occasionally flutter her lashes'; now, however, she was displaying 'a rich personality' and 'racing to the top in America'.

Fig. 3: The Secret People.

Fig. 4: Roman Holiday.

The third promotion: Cinderella in Hollywood
In Paramount's promotion, Hepburn was no longer offered primarily as an object for male fantasies about the sexual availability of young women. Instead her performances and the accompanying publicity presented her as an object of identification for women. Her Cinderella-like transformation from starlet to superstar was the focus of numerous press reports about the success of *Gigi* which ran on Broadway until 31 May 1952, about her tumultuous reception by the press in Rome where she arrived in June 1952 for the shooting of *Roman Holiday*, and about the sustained publicity campaign itself that Paramount conducted for its latest star, preparing the public for the film's release in August 1953 with the promise of the greatest discovery since Garbo.

Hepburn's life was depicted as a young woman's dream, or a fairy tale, come true. Her role in *Roman Holiday* was seen as that of a fairy-tale princess, the story described as 'Cinderella in reverse'. At the same time the film's trailer emphasized how new the actress was to stardom and how her real reward was to be close to, and have a fun time with, Hollywood idol Gregory Peck who played the American journalist with whom the princess spends her day (see Figure 4).

In interviews Hepburn also discussed the hard work and crushing sense of responsibility that stardom entailed. This culminated in the cancellation of her engagement

Fig. 5 & 6: Roman Holiday.

with Hanson in December 1952. As some reviewers observed at the time, in the same way that the actress cannot combine career and romance, in the film Princess Ann, out of a sense of responsibility for her people, ends her romantic involvement with Peck's reporter to return to her royal duties.

All that Ann can take away from this experience are her memories and a few snap-shots of her Roman holiday. One of the major selling points of the film was the fact that it gave its audiences privileged access to historic Roman sites as well as to the contemporary lifestyle of Roman youth, creating a sense of participation rather than merely providing a tourist's outside view. This is not so much a case of selling Europe to American audiences, but a genuine attempt at representing Europe to the Europeans. After all, the duties that Princess Ann carries out at the beginning and returns to at the end of the film, include her support for a European federation and the intensification of trade relations between European countries, issues of striking topicality in early 1950s Europe. The opening fake newsreel about the princess's goodwill tour begins to con-struct the image of a Western Europe in the process of economic and perhaps cultural integration. Royalty is celebrated in every capital, providing a kind of trans-European cultural currency (as, indeed, do American films such as *Roman Holiday*). The newsreel also cements Audrey Hepburn's star status: The way in which Princess Ann is celebrated by crowds all over Europe invites comparison with the adulation and mass hysteria that the greatest film stars are able to provoke, as we see in this shot-reverse-shot cutting between actual crowds on the border of hysteria and Princess Ann smiling at her fans from her state-like carriage (see Figures 5 and 6).

Later press reports about Hepburn remarked on the overwhelming reaction of the public to her personal appearances. Rather than belonging to any one nation, Hepburn, just as Princess Ann, belonged to Europe. Indeed, the press response to her break-through shows that she was proudly claimed as a former British starlet by the British and as the offspring of a Dutch aristocratic family by the Dutch. In both cases, the loss

The Making of an International Star:
The Early Film Career and Star Image of Audrey Hepburn, 1948–54
Peter Krämer

Fig. 7: Sabrina.

of this national treasure to Hollywood was mourned, yet it was also acknowledged that only Hollywood had the resources to establish her as an international star.

It could be argued, then, that with its topicality, its Roman setting and its Belgian-Dutch-English female lead, *Roman Holiday* constituted a conscious effort to appeal to European audiences. While there was a necessity for Paramount and other Hollywood companies to invest frozen capital accumulated in European countries in so-called runaway productions, these also made good sense in marketing terms. Cinema audiences in the United States were declining rapidly while attendances in European movie theatres were increasing (with the exception of Britain). Since European audiences preferred domestic products to American imports, Hollywood increasingly used stars, locations and subject matter which connected with the national cultures of various European countries. Audrey Hepburn's film career is probably the most striking example of this policy. In her subsequent films she often played European characters engaging with aspects of European culture, starting with her Cinderella role in *Sabrina*. Here, she is the English chauffeur's daughter, who gets an education and a spectacular wardrobe (designed by couturier Hubert de Givenchy) in Paris, which helps her to win the heart of the heir to the extensive business of the family that employs her father (see Figure 6). *Sabrina* ends with the union of Hepburn's Cinderella and Bogart's American business tycoon. This union takes place on an ocean liner on the way to Europe.

In another instance of life imitating art (which again was remarked upon in contemporary reports), after the shooting of *Sabrina* in the autumn of 1953, Hepburn completed her second successful run on Broadway, playing the water-sprite in *Ondine* (Alfred Lunt) opposite American film star Mel Ferrer, with whom she became romantically involved and took back to Europe on an ocean liner in the summer of 1954, where she married him around the time of *Sabrina*'s release in September 1954. Both on and off the screen, then, Audrey Hepburn brought the peoples of Europe and North America together. ●

~~~~~~~~~~~~~~

GO FURTHER

Extracts/Essays/Articles

'Opportunity Knocked for Audrey Hepburn and Veronica Hurst', ABPC press release from 1950, on Audrey Hepburn fiche no. 1, British Film Institute.

Sunday Chronicle, 1 April 1951, untitled and unpaginated clipping on Audrey Hepburn fiche no.1, British Film Institute.

Evening News, 10 March 1951, untitled and unpaginated clipping on Audrey Hepburn fiche no.1, British Film Institute.

Donald Leo, 'A New Girl Steps into British Pictures', *Daily Mirror*, 23 January 1952, unpaginated clipping on Audrey Hepburn fiche no. 1, British Film Institute.

Chapter
8

Little Black Dress: Audrey, Fashion and Fans

Armen Karaoghlanian

→ The arrival of Audrey Hepburn in Hollywood was very much instantaneous. In 1954, after making her grand entrance in Hollywood with her first starring role in a major motion picture as a princess in *Roman Holiday* (William Wyler, 1953), she won an Oscar at the young age of 24.

Fig. 1: Princess Ann rides around Rome with Joe Bradley, seeking freedom and independence from her sheltered lifestyle.

The world curiously watched this young unknown actress transform into a star, as she quickly became an icon for both the motion picture industry and fashion industry.

Let's take a Roman holiday!
In her breakthrough film, *Roman Holiday*, a young Audrey Hepburn captivated her audience with her exceptional sense of charm, elegance and innocence. The world was introduced to a new kind of star. In comparison to the voluptuous, curvy blonde stars of the time, she was scrawny, boyish and slim. Billy Wilder, who directed her in *Sabrina* (1954) and *Love in the Afternoon* (1957) humorously observed (quoted by Barry Paris), 'If that girl had tits, she could rule the world.' The fact that she was so different from other stars of this time period also helped set her apart from the crowd.

In *Roman Holiday*, and many other films throughout her career, she went against the usual image for stars of the time period and was admired by audiences for her individuality and fashion sense rather than her looks. The young actress also displayed her interest in fashion with the film by occasionally accessorizing with scarves that complemented her costumes. In a particular scene, where her character sneaks into a barbershop and cuts off her long hair, she epitomized youthful independence. The role

Little Black Dress: Audrey, Fashion and Fans
Armen Karaoghlanian

Fig. 2: Billy Wilder gives Givenchy an introduction he deserves, introducing Sabrina through her clothing.

of a sheltered princess, who seeks escape from her routine lifestyle, resonated with audiences around the world. The premiere of *Roman Holiday* at the Radio City Music Hall in New York was around the time when *Sabrina* was getting ready for production. The success of the film – particularly Audrey Hepburn's Oscar win – created a star out of the young actress. In a short amount of time, she became the centre of attention, and her sense of style and fashion became the focus of discussion.

The Givenchy girl
Sabrina was a turning point in Audrey's career in terms of fashion because her lifelong collaboration with fashion designer Hubert de Givenchy was born. Audrey Hepburn's recently acquired fame meant that she could now have contractual demands, and in keeping up with her interest in fashion, she requested that she pick a fashion designer for her costumes for *Sabrina*. The first choice she had was Cristóbal Balenciaga, who was working in Paris. The legendary designer was unavailable, and so he recommended Hubert de Givenchy, his protégé and a former apprentice of Elsa Schiaparelli.

Fig. 3: Sabrina's stunning gown was one of the three dresses the actress initially picked when she visited Givenchy in Paris.

Givenchy had been known for style, grace and minimalism in his designs. Givenchy's first encounter with Audrey was in Paris's 18th arrondissement. The story goes that when Givenchy was notified that a Miss Hepburn had arrived for him, he assumed the actress in question was Katharine Hepburn. This was because Audrey was still relatively unknown in France in the early 1950s. In *Edith Head: The Fifty-Year Career of Hollywood's Greatest Costume Designer*, Jay Jorgensen notes Givenchy's first impression of her. 'I was at first surprised ... almost disappointed!' remembers the designer. In describing the actress, he notes that she was a 'young woman, very slim, very tall, with doe eyes and short hair and wearing a pair of narrow pants, a little T-shirt, slippers and a gondolier's hat with red ribbon that read "Venezia"'.

Givenchy was busy working on his new collection at the time of her arrival and was therefore unavailable to design costumes specifically for her. Audrey Hepburn instead selected three dresses from his boutique that were already designed and wore them in the film. The designs received a considerable amount of praise, which resulted in a life-long relationship and friendship between designer and actress that lasted four decades. In their respective careers, she became his muse and he became her guide.

In the first portion of the film, Sabrina is seen wearing unglamorous outfits. These costume choices are directly contrasted with her clothing when she arrives back in town

Figure 4: Audrey Hepburn added her sense of style to the Givenchy costumes. In this intimate scene with Humphrey Bogart, she has accessorized her dress with a fashionable hat.

from Paris, where she reinvents herself. It's after her arrival when we see her draped in Givenchy's stunning dresses. The director of the film, Billy Wilder, gives Givenchy a grand introduction. Sabrina, after having arrived from Paris, is introduced with a slow pan up, carefully revealing every inch of her dress. The careful reveal isn't just because she has changed throughout the course of the film, but it's also an indication of the real-life Audrey Hepburn, who has transformed into a fashion icon.

The Givenchy designs were unique in the sense they placed less emphasis on the physical features of women. The actress and designer complimented each other's work and became models for elegance and grace that would be imitated for decades to come.

There was no legal obligation on the part of Paramount Pictures to credit Givenchy because a contract did not exist between him and the studio. Edith Head received sole credit on the film, and after her fourth Oscar win in 1955, she failed to mention or thank Givenchy. The fact that Givenchy was cheated out of a screen credit for his work in *Sabrina* was disheartening for Audrey Hepburn. The actress made clear that from this point on, her contracts would include a clause stating that Givenchy would design her film clothes and receive proper credit for his work. In *Funny Face* (Stanley Donen, 1957), the credits boldly read, 'Miss Hepburn's Paris Wardrobe by Hubert de Givenchy.'

Audrey also continued her collaboration with fashion designer Salvatore Ferragamo, who had originally worked with her during *Roman Holiday*. The Italian designer, who had originally designed shoes for his sisters in his homeland, enrolled at the University of Southern California and studied metatarsal anatomy as a way of discovering why his shoes were uncomfortable despite being aesthetically pleasing. The shoes he designed for Audrey Hepburn in *Sabrina* later became known as the Sabrina heel, further emphasizing her influence in the fashion. In addition to her influence within the fashion industry along with Givenchy's guidance, Audrey was also signalling a shift in our taste in women during this time period. *Photoplay* (quoted by Barry Paris), one of the first film fan magazines in the United States, accurately described her as 'flat-chested, slim hipped and altogether un-Marilyn Monroeish'. *Silver Screen* asked after the release of *Sabrina*: 'Is Hollywood shifting its accent on sex? She's changing Hollywood's taste in girls.' The general public had now fully embraced her charming, sophisticated European look over the typical artificiality of Hollywood bombshells. In November 1954, Cecil Beaton of *Vogue* rightfully pointed out that Audrey was transforming the concept of beauty and was sparking imitations throughout the nation. The young star had represented the new feminine ideal and everyone in town was now observing and recording her every move.

The girl with the funny face

In terms of an inexperienced amateur being thrown into a world of fame, *Funny Face*

Little Black Dress: Audrey, Fashion and Fans
Armen Karaoghlanian

Figure 5: Jo Stockton (Audrey Hepburn) poses for a photograph in Funny Face, as she wears a Givenchy designed hat.

very much resembles Audrey's own life. The character of Jo Stockton (Audrey Hepburn) resembles her early life before her glamour. Jo remarks, 'I have no illusions about my looks. I think my face is funny.' The fact that Jo Stockton goes from unfashionable clerk to the fashionista model she becomes in the film is further suggestive of the real-life Audrey Hepburn, as, despite her beauty, Audrey's face is 'funny' in its defiance of bland convention. The supporting characters and plot points in the film also reference her world as well. The magazine publisher where Dick Avery (Fred Astaire) works as a fashion photographer, 'Quality', is clearly a reference to *Vogue*, whereas the fashion designer that Jo works with in Paris is a reference to Givenchy.

Funny Face was a notable film for a number of reasons. The film assured Givenchy would be credited for his designs from now on. The film further emphasized that Audrey Hepburn had arrived – despite the fact that the film was originally developed for Fred Astaire, a veteran of cinema at this point in his career, Audrey Hepburn received credit billing over him. In addition, it was with this film that she began asserting control over her costume choices while collaborating with other members of her team. As noted by Jay Jorgensen, Edith Head remarked that she 'had an adorable sweetness that made you feel like a mother getting her only daughter ready for prom' and that she 'could have been a designer herself, she had such perfect taste'.

Audrey Hepburn understood the essentials of fashion – she believed in underdressing rather than overdressing – and knew she could use accessories, colours and clothing choices as a way of complimenting her physical appearance and accentuating parts of her body. In her personal and professional life, for instance, she began exclusively wearing flats as a way of deemphasizing her height.

In fact, she was extremely self-conscious and insecure about her physical appearance – her mother even jokingly called her an 'ugly duckling' – and she often avoided smiling because of the unevenness of her teeth. In *It's So Audrey: A Style Icon*, Sean Ferrer, her son with Mel Ferrer, believed that even though his mother would only see her flaws, she was the 'perfect package of imperfections'. In his belief, the very 'definition of beauty is not knowing that you are so special'. These insecurities, however, never discouraged her and she accepted her shortcomings; during the filming of *Roman Holiday*, the studio offered to cap her teeth and pluck her thick eyebrows, but she curiously declined their offer. The star believed in being practical and 'facing your

Fig. 6: Audrey Hepburn transformed into a beautiful, simple bride as she wore a wedding dress in Funny Face that was, of course, designed by Givenchy.

handicaps' rather than hiding away from imperfections, which is why her eyebrows essentially became a part of her image. There was never anything artificial about her; she bought shoes half a size too big, for instance, because she felt that cramming her feet into shoes meant they wouldn't last as long, and in her later years, when she began greying, she avoided colouring her hair. Audrey embraced her body and image throughout her career and became an icon for doing so.

Funny Face further continued her friendship with Givenchy. In Audrey Hepburn, Barry Paris notes Audrey Hepburn as having said, 'I depend on Givenchy [...] There are few people I love more.'. Their collaboration brought immense success onto Givenchy's sales. In their imitation of their favourite star, women rushed to his salon and sales began rising for the designer. Audrey Hepburn was clearly influencing the fashion world just as much as she had influenced the film industry.

Just in time for breakfast

The role Audrey Hepburn is most remembered for is also the one she believed she was miscast in. The star played against type for the film as a working girl. Truman Capote, the author of the novella, Breakfast at Tiffany's (1958), had advocated for Marilyn Monroe. The fact that Audrey landed the part is further suggestive of the notion that tastes were changing in female actresses. In the film, she dons a simple black dress that was designed by Givenchy. The dress, and her character, Holly Golightly, became an icon for film and fashion, respectively. The original 'little black dress', along with the belief that every woman should own a simple black dress, were created by Coco Chanel in 1926. The dress is now universally considered one of the most influential garments in the fashion industry, largely because Audrey Hepburn became a visual representation of that idea.

The dress Audrey Hepburn wears in the opening scene is a satin evening gown with long black gloves, strands of pearls and a tiara. The success of Breakfast at Tiffany's brought about a transformation of Audrey Hepburn as a star, as her youthful presence in the 1950s evolved into the sophisticated trendsetter of the 1960s.

The trendsetter

In her later career, as her style evolved with her age, she began enlisting the assistance

Little Black Dress: Audrey, Fashion and Fans
Armen Karaoghlanian

Fig. 7: The famous opening scene of Breakfast at Tiffany's (Blake Edwards, 1961), in which Audrey Hepburn, as Holly Golightly, stands outside of Tiffany's in her little black dress.

of new designers. The star never abandoned Givenchy, however, but she did naturally begin exploring other options. The star began seeking new designers while living in Rome and stumbled upon Valentino Garavani, a young dressmaker making a name for himself in Italy. Ralph Lauren was another designer she collaborated with because of his casual clothing. Their first encounter came in his New York flagship store on Seventy-Second Street and Madison Avenue. Ralph Lauren, unlike Givenchy, was a huge admirer when he first met her. The designer claims Audrey asked for his autograph upon meeting him. In *Audrey Hepburn* by Parris (author Brian Paris), we learn that Ralph Lauren exclaimed, 'I wanted *her* autograph!'

The evolution of her fashion sense became obvious in later films throughout the 1960s and 1970s. The costumes in her films were always under Givenchy's direction and were reflective of changing times. In *Charade* (Stanley Donen, 1963), she is entirely chic, as she wears collarless jackets and pillbox hats. In *How to Steal a Million* (William Wyler, 1966), she is both retro and modern, adapting to the evolving fashion styles of the late 1960s, but at the same time, adding her sense of style to the character's outfits. In *Two for the Road* (Stanley Donen, 1967), she further experimented with styles, wearing designers such as Mary Quant and Paco Rabanne. In the film, she dons everything from a psychedelic mini-dress to the green zipper pull jacket with her oversized white sunglasses.

In her mini-series documentary, *Gardens of the World with Audrey Hepburn* (Bruce Franchini, 1993), she approached Ralph Lauren, stating, 'I love Givenchy for night, but I love your sport clothes for daytime.' The collaboration with Ralph Lauren proved, above all, that Audrey Hepburn remained loyal with Givenchy and depended on other designers based on specific looks. Their work together showed, more than anything, that Givenchy's designs were for special occasions that the actress attended, such as tributes and receptions, whereas Ralph Lauren's designs were for practical events and outings. Ralph Lauren, more than anyone else, was aware of her importance in his life. In *Audrey Hepburn* by Barry Paris, he states, 'She did more for the designer than the designer did for her.'

That's so Audrey!
In her career, she became an icon of film and fashion. In Audrey Hepburn, Barry Paris

Fig. 8: Audrey Hepburn keeps up with the evolving fashion trends of the 1960s as she opts for oversized white sunglasses and a green zipper pull jacket.

notes that 'in the sixties as in the fifties [...] she virtually *defined* the feminine vogues of the decade'. In fact, she has become such an influential force that her name has become an adjective within the world of fashion. 'That's so Audrey!' is now shorthand for a clean, modern and sophisticated look. The influence she had on the world included more than just the general public. In her time, and even until recent years, celebrities continuously consider her an inspiration. In a letter to the famed actress (quoted by Barry Paris), Cher wrote the following:

I so wanted to be like you in *Breakfast at Tiffany's* that I put my hair in two ponytails, bought huge sunglasses, and wore the closest thing to 'you' I could put together. I got suspended from school for the sunglasses.

Salvatore Ferragamo's shoes for Audrey Hepburn in *Sabrina* are now named after the actress and are continuous best sellers for the company. The shoes that she wore simply as a way of deemphasizing her height have now caught on with the world.

The rule for Audrey Hepburn's wardrobe was always quality over quantity. The essentials of her wardrobe always consisted of a little black dress, white blouse, sophisticated suits, Capri pants, black sweaters, oversized sunglasses, a scarf, ballet-slipper flats, little or no jewellery and pale shades of lipstick. These became the ingredients of one of the most influential fashion icons of the world. Audrey Hepburn was a star known for her sense of style and infectious sense of charm. In her early career, she became a symbol for independence and she soon became a symbol for confidence as she continuously embraced her unique image. Billy Wilder (quoted by Barry Paris) remarked that 'Audrey was known for something which has disappeared, and this is elegance, grace and manners'.

The arrival of Audrey Hepburn in Hollywood may have been instantaneous, but her influence in both fashion and film has endured for decades. ●

Little Black Dress: Audrey, Fashion and Fans
Armen Karaoghlanian

~~~~~~~~~~~

GO FURTHER

Books

100 Years of Fashion
Cally Blackman
(London: Laurence King, 2012)

Audrey Hepburn: International Cover Girl
Scott Brizel
(San Francisco, CA: Chronicle, 2009)

Audrey Hepburn: A Life in Pictures.
Yann-Brice Dherbier
(London: Pavilion, 2008)

Edith Head: The Fifty-year Career of Hollywood's Greatest Costume Designer
Jay Jorgensen
(Philadelphia: Running, 2010)

Audrey Style
Pamela Clarke Keogh and Hubert De Givenchy
(London: Aurum, 1999)

Audrey Hepburn
Barry Paris
(New York: Putnam, 1996)

Extracts/Essays/Articles
Silver Screen, Earl Wilson, July, 1954.

'I HAVE MORE SEX APPEAL
ON THE TIP OF MY NOSE
THAN MANY WOMEN HAVE
IN THEIR ENTIRE BODIES. IT
DOESN'T STAND OUT A MILE,
BUT IT IS THERE'.

AUDREY HEPBURN

Chapter
9

The Audrey Hat Trick

Francis Vose

→ Designer speak – 'That's so Audrey': clean line, modern look, a look that works – shorthand for something stylish, tasteful and always works. Her friend and director Peter Bogdanovich is quoted on Fashion Capital website as saying: 'Audrey's charm is like the Mona Lisa. You can't define it; you can only experience it.' Iconic images stay with you and become influential in style, time and memories. They touch you and give you a feeling about that person and about that look that we connect with.

As with many iconic Hollywood stars Audrey Hepburn created a dream, but her classic beauty keeps her alive today. On- and off-screen, she wore simple but stylish dresses, hats and accessories which emphasized her feminine charm. Famous for the classic 'little black dress' in *Breakfast at Tiffany's* (Blake Edwards, 1961), to the celebrated title of 'Cap Queen' for the variety of iconic hats that dominated her screen image. Audrey Hepburn became one of the most famous fashion icons ever. Her style, charm and grace; her 'clean line, modern look, a look that always works', is still being celebrated and imitated today.

I have been involved in design all my working life and have always aimed to look for the ordinary as well as the extraordinary. Sometimes the ordinary can be extraordinary. A cloud in the sky; an elephant riding a motorbike. A spill of oil in a puddle; a map of the world. A solitary tree; an 'Audrey hat'. I have always loved hats, but an 'Audrey hat' is something to behold.

In 2004, Cosgrove Hall Films, Europe's leading animation company, were commissioned by Northern & Shell (owner of the *Daily Express* newspaper) to develop their Rupert the Bear brand. As the Creative Director of Cosgrove Hall Films it was my task to develop the Rupert brand and create a children's television series that would continue to capture the hearts of millions of children and help take Rupert seamlessly into the twenty-first century. My vision was to remain true to the original character but develop a new brand that could build upon its heritage. I have designed, developed and produced a great number of commercially successful award winning projects for television and retail spanning more than thirty years, including Postman Pat, The Wind in the Willows, Little Robots and Bill and Ben to name but a few, and I knew how important the task was to 'get it right'.

I grew up with Rupert the Bear and was occasionally bought the annuals at Christmas, but I was never a true fan.

Fig. 1: Rupert Bear Annuals 1953 and 1959 © Northern & Shell.

The Audrey Hat Trick
Francis Vose

I liked Rupert Bear; probably because he was a 'teddy' bear, but I found the world he lived in rather unsettling. The human characters never really sat well with me and I found his adventures terribly old-fashioned.

Fig. 2: Alfred Bestall's illustrations 1960 © Northern & Shell.

The stories and design for the annuals produced for today's market still remain very traditional.

Fig. 3: Rupert Bear Annuals 1985 (50th) and 2011 (75th) © Northern & Shell.

The brief from Northern & Shell was to develop a major new Rupert Bear television series to implement a full consumer products campaign and DVD release programme for the brand. My first task was to research everything about Rupert, including the previous television series, merchandise and marketing campaigns. I discovered that most of the material produced was derived from the original drawn material from creator Mary Tourtel or from the Rupert the Bear annuals and television series which are based on Alfred Bestall's illustrations.

First published in 1920, Rupert the Bear is still going strong and recognized by many as an iconic children's character almost as famous for his trademark yellow check scarf and trousers as Audrey continues to be for her little black dresses; however unlikely it

*Fig. 4: John Harrold 1993,
20th Century Unattributed
illustration 1985, and Royal
Doulton figure 2004
© Northern & Shell.*

might sound, they are both sartorial legends, and in an era where the platform for global opportunities is unlimited drawing on links to the Audrey Hepburn 'brand' cannot be ignored.

*Fig. 5: Alfred Bestall illustra-
tion 1970 © Northern & Shell.*

I knew that if I was to make an impact in a highly competitive children's television market that is driven by the exploitation of a brand for its investment return, I knew I had to come up with something different but was also aware how important it was that the 'new' Rupert should remain true to the original character and his surroundings of Nutwood village.

My research led me to think that Rupert the Bear was like a 10-year-old boy with a bear's head.

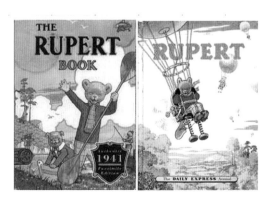

*Fig. 6: Rupert Bear Annuals
1941 and 1957 © Northern &
Shell.*

The Audrey Hat Trick
Francis Vose

His adventures were exciting, colourful and sometimes quite odd, but were adventures that 10-year-old boys would not be having or be interested in for the twenty-first century.

Fig. 7: © Nelvana Limited Inc.1991-1997 (an international division Corus Entertainment).

Taking this into consideration I made the decision to re-develop the 10-year-old boy/bear into a pre-school television series and re-age him as a 5-year-old Bear.

Fig. 8: Rupert – original puppet from the television series Rupert Bear: Follow the Magic... © Entertainment Rights. Classic Media. Boomerang Media. DreamWorks Classics (Mary Tourtel and Alfred Bestall, Channel 5, 2006-present)

The 5-year-old Rupert would offer access to the wonderful imaginative land of the original story structure but open new doors to an exciting world for the modern pre-school child. As with many other children's series I have developed and created I began work on Rupert's environment and surroundings first. I decided to lose all the human characters and the shop/street settings from the original Nutwood village and concentrate on Rupert and his close friends; the wooded areas of Nutwood including Rupert's house, a coast line and a lighthouse.

My research of British woodland and coastlines were extensive (I probably took longer than I really needed, but the seaside is my favourite place to be). I had a very clear

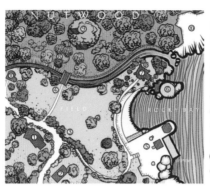

Fig. 9: Original Nutwood map design for Rupert Bear: Follow the Magic... © Entertainment Rights. Classic Media. Boomerang Media. DreamWorks Animation (2006-present).

① RUPERT'S COTTAGE AND GARDEN
② EDWARD TRUNK'S HOUSE
③ POSTBOX AND SIGNPOST
④ BRIDGE
⑤ ROCKY BAY LIGHTHOUSE
⑥ MERMAID ROCKS
⑦ PING PONG'S PAGODA
⑧ FOX TWINS SET
⑨ THE TREE HOUSE AND RAGGETY's HOUSE
⑩ CLIFFS AND CAVES
⑪ BILL BADGERS HOUSE

idea about the design concept, but I needed it to be visualized for my design team to understand my direction and thought process. My favourite tree is the silver birch and I was very keen to use the texture of the bark and feature the simple white structure of the trunks, but the foliage of the silver birch was a little fussy for my design so I started to research more uniformed shapes like clipped box and topiary. This helped me consider the design from an outline and silhouette perspective. On one of my many visits to the coast and woodland I visited Formby in the Metropolitan Borough of Sefton, in Merseyside, a coastline with a fantastic landscape of sea and sand dunes. It is famous for the red squirrel sanctuary run by the National Trust which is set in a pine forest close to the coastline. Perfect for my research!

My eureka moment!

My research had gone well and I had a good selection of images to show my team but I hadn't got the image or the hook that I knew I would need to explain my thoughts precisely. Rupert was easy; he is now a 5-year-old cute and cuddly bear for a pre-school market with his iconic scarf, checked trousers and a red jumper but his world needed to be as simple to explain and illustrate. As I walked out of the red squirrel forest towards the coast I saw my image. I excitedly pulled my camera to my eye and said 'Audrey hat'.

Fig. 10: Solitary Audrey tree – Formby 2005 © Francis Vose.

The Audrey Hat Trick
Francis Vose

The image was of a cluster of windswept pine trees and one stand alone tree in the shape of an Audrey Hepburn hat. Graphic design is all about the outline. Fashion is all about the silhouette. I had found the hook.
It incorporated everything I had been researching in one image. A long thin trunk with a topiary-style top to it.
    I now knew what to tell my team – 'Nutwood will look like a sea of Audrey Hepburn hats.'

Fig. 11: Original set designs for Rupert Bear: Follow the Magic... © Entertainment Rights. Classic Media. Boomerang Media. DreamWorks Animation (2006-present).

    The trunks will be textured and coloured like a silver birch and the foliage will look like an Audrey hat.

Fig. 12: Original set designs for Rupert Bear: Follow the Magic... © Entertainment Rights. Classic Media. Boomerang Media. DreamWorks Animation (2006-present).

I had a team of young and old, with different points of view and very different film and fashion interests, but when I told them that Nutwood's trees will look like Audrey Hepburn hats, they all got it – every single one of them!

Fig. 13: Original set designs for Rupert Bear: Follow the Magic… © Entertainment Rights. Classic Media. Boomerang Media. DreamWorks Animation (2006-present).

It was crucial to maintain a focus throughout the development of the series and vital that the brand remained true to its roots and relevant to a new audience, but throughout a lengthy development and production period it is so easy to lose sight of the purpose of the product which can lead to the design losing its focus, therefore I decided to adopt an easy-to-remember quote from Audrey – Nothing is impossible; the word itself says 'I'm possible'! It made staying on brand throughout the production so easy – if someone came off product, they were reminded to 'think Audrey'.

Fig. 14: Original set designs for Rupert Bear: Follow the Magic… © Entertainment Rights. Classic Media. Boomerang Media. DreamWorks Animation (2006-present).

In such a difficult financial climate where advertising in children's television, DVD sales, bespoke apparel and toys are on the decline, many producers have to adopt a quick production turnaround and an even quicker return for their massive outlay invested, but a classic show like *The Adventures of Rupert Bear* (Mary Tourtel, ITV, 1969-1977) needed careful handling. I had deliberated long and hard over the design and style of the series and was keen to uphold the quality throughout every design process and maintain a constant sophisticated look. Therefore the detailing of each element of the brand design, including, market research, production design and toy manufacturing,

Fig. 15: An array of
Audrey hats

was meticulously considered.

The shared characteristics of Audrey Hepburn and Rupert Bear are not obvious, and the probability of both brands having a shared cultural view may have proved implausible. But simple design qualities, clean lines and a modern look have proved uncannily similar.

Audrey had breakfast at Tiffany's. I wanted a feast in Harvey Nichols. I aimed for style, class and sophistication. In short – I thought Audrey!

Rupert Bear: Follow the Magic... became an instant hit with pre-school children and their mums and dads, and a leading global brand with significant merchandising product, including a tree house in the shape of an Audrey hat. ●

GO FURTHER

Online

http://www.fashioncapital.co.uk/News/25188-Thats-so-Audrey.html

Fig. 16: Rupert Bear: Follow the Magic... logo and publicity shot © Entertainment Rights. Classic Media. Boomerang Media. DreamWorks Animation (2006-present).

Fig. 17: Rupert Tree House Playset © Entertainment Rights. Classic Media. Boomerang Media. DreamWorks Animation (2007).

Chapter
10

Audrey Hepburn Syndrome: It's a Girl (and Sometimes a Boy) Thing

Jacqui Miller

→ **Audrey Hepburn continues to be the star who has by far the most extensive and multi-layered persona in popular culture, as well as the most loved. Sure, Elvis is still an icon, but he is often seen as a figure of fun, a cheese-burger scoffing glutton. Marilyn Monroe remains a byword for glamour, but her style is unwearable for the modern woman, and would anyone really want to emulate her pills and booze-fuddled lifestyle?**

Audrey continues to have a cultural presence that is extended on a literally daily basis. Leafing through issue 393 of *Grazia* yesterday (14 August 2012) I contemplated buying online fashion company Boohoo's black Audrey bag, while today I was tempted by Joules's Audrey tunic dress. Sadly, Boden's beautiful Audrey coat has sold out in my size, as has their Audrey print shift, but the Audrey dress from the new autumn/winter collection is available. And it is not only the 'English classics' companies such as Boden and Joules, which sell clothes we might imagine Audrey herself buying, that use her name. Online store, Rockabilly Pinup are now selling the 'Audrey Black Dress' by Glamour Bunny. This 'gorgeous pinup dress' is quite unlike her typical style, but the association of the 'Audrey' name with a 'black dress' evokes an irresistible aura.

But Audrey's presence is not just felt in fashion. Whether it is television, films, online, self-help, fiction – any medium where women have fun together, Audrey can be found. At the London 2012 Olympic Games opening ceremony my Facebook status was hot with messages from friends as we exclaimed over spotting the *Breakfast at Tiffany's* (Blake Edwards, 1961) kiss in the rain. When chatting on Facebook with a fellow Audrey fan our profile pictures taken from Audrey's films make it seem as if her various on-screen personae are in debate with each other. And, unlike Elvis or Marilyn, it is always in a good way; Audrey is never a figure of fun and she is *always* a lady. Why is this so, almost sixty years since her stardom burst onto the world? The answer may be partly found by returning to the Boden website. Typing 'Audrey' into 'search results' does not just produce the clothes mentioned above; their 'elegant coat' appears too. Biographies celebrate her charm in titles including her son, Sean Ferrer's *Audrey Hepburn: Elegant Spirit* (2005); Ian Woodward's *Audrey Hepburn: Fair Lady of the Screen* (1993); and Donald Spoto's *Enchantment: The Life of Audrey Hepburn* (2006). In a world in which elegance seems to be an increasingly limited commodity, we rely on Audrey for its continued diffusion, and this chapter will explore the ways in which all things associated with Audrey sprinkle stardust across female (and sometimes male) culture and provide inspiration to us all.

Breakfast at Tiffany's: I Heart NY
Of all Audrey's film roles, Holly Golightly in *Breakfast at Tiffany's* is by far the most influential and is central in a web of female cultural references that stretch backwards to the nineteenth and forwards to the twenty-first centuries. Holly could be an early 1960s version of an Edith Wharton character. Like *The House of Mirth*'s (1905) impoverished but beautiful and charming Lily Bart, Holly knows by heart the exact place of every man on America's rich list and is delighted when the ninth place, Rusty Trawler, shows up at her party. Also like Lily, once Holly has decided she is to be 'a *jeune fille à marier*', she dedicates herself to trapping her prey: while Lily uses even a casual conversation to learn about the Americana beloved of Percy Gryce, Holly swots up on Jose da Silva Pereira's (Jose Luis De Villalonga) wealth in the public library, a place she had previously

Audrey Hepburn Syndrome: It's a Girl (and Sometimes a Boy) Thing
Jacqui Miller

Fig. 1: Samantha can't resist the prospect of breakfast with his Tiffanies.

eschewed. Similarly, despite scrupulous early preparation, subsequent careless behaviour (in Lily's case, a walk with Lawrence Selden, in Holly's, unwitting intelligence for Sally Tomato [Alan Reed]), always prevents her gaining her 'prize'. In Candace Bushnell's 1997 collected essays, *Sex and the City*, the narrator acknowledges the similarity between Wharton's and modern-day New York's women, and the HBO television series continued the intertextuality by making several implicit and explicit references to Holly and to *Breakfast at Tiffany's*. The very first episode of Season 1, screened in 1998, opens with Carrie Bradshaw (Sarah Jessica Parker) narrating: 'Once upon a time' before telling the audience a rather depressing account of an attractive female English journalist who has come to New York, been romanced by an apparently eligible bachelor in his early forties but after being asked to look at a house with him and meet his parents, is dumped. Carrie continues:

Welcome to the age of un-innocence. No one has breakfast at Tiffany's and no one has affairs to remember. Instead we have breakfast at 7 a.m. and affairs we try to forget as quickly as possible. Self-protection and closing the deal are paramount.

We can see at once how associations with Audrey and her era underline the contrast with the grubbiness of today. 'Once upon a time' sets the fairy-tale tone of Audrey's life and film plots, and this is emphasized by the implied reference to the romantic weepie *An Affair to Remember* (Leo McCarey, 1957) but especially to *Breakfast at Tiffany's* – there is even a cheeky in-joke to the fans, Paramount being the *Tiffany's* producing studio. But this lustrous life has been lost today: 'the age of un-innocence' ironicizes the title of one of Wharton's best-known books, *The Age of Innocence* (1905), filmed in 1993 by Martin Scorsese.

Throughout the six seasons, Tiffany's, through its associations with Holly/Audrey, casts magic and the store features in Sex and the City tours of New York. As we see in Figure 1, in Season 3, Episode 5, sex-pot Samantha (Kim Cattrall) breaks her usual no-sleepover rule and invites a blinged-up lover to stay so she can have 'breakfast with his Tiffanies'.

In Season 4, Episode 17, there are tensions between Miranda (Samantha Nixon) and Charlotte (Miranda is a single-parent to be, focused on her career as a high-flying lawyer and ambivalent about motherhood, while Charlotte, separated from her husband and longing for a child herself, vicariously organizes a lavish baby-shower for the reluctant Miranda).

As the presents are unwrapped, a distinctive blue box signals a classy gift. As we see in Figure 1, Charlotte is overcome as Miranda opens a silver rattle just like one her husband had bought for her before she miscarried their child. However, just as Tiffany's was

a panacea for Holly's 'mean reds', this gift brings Charlottes emotions out cathartically, but also forces Miranda to recognize her own qualms about motherhood and the two friends are truly reconciled. But it is the Season 4 finale, episode 18, that most lovingly evokes the spirit of Audrey. Mr Big is on the verge of leaving Manhattan for California and is visited at his apartment by Carrie. Leafing through his record collection, she finds a Mancini album that belonged to his parents. Modern New York is transformed into a romantic oasis as 'Moon River' (Henry Mancini, 1961) plays. Big describes his parents listening to the song as they got ready for Saturday night parties and he and Carrie dance. As we see in Figures 3 and 4, in a T-shirt and pedal pushers, her hair in a ponytail, Carrie channels Holly/Audrey's dressed-down style, her own twist added by trademark heels.

The episode goes on to play to fans' knowledge of the book and film. On the eve of her journey to Brazil, the book's Holly goes horseback riding in Central Park, ending with her being thrown and miscarrying her baby. In the episode, it is Big who is leaving town, and rather than horseback riding they take a horse-drawn carriage through the park; the ride turns into a gallop because Carrie needs to fulfil her duties as Miranda's birthing partner. This baby is born safely and *Breakfast at Tiffany's* has evoked a kind of fairly tale for today's New York girls. Indeed, this episode, 'I Heart New York' reflects Holly's words 'I love New York' in its post 9/11 dedication 'to our city of New York, then, now and forever'.

What would Audrey do?

Just as *Sex and the City* merges Audrey and Holly into a magic wand of feminine charm, so does a type of book, part style guide, part self-help manual that is uniquely associated with Audrey. Some, such as *Audrey Style* (1999), concentrate on fashion, while others, including *What Would Audrey Do? Timeless Lessons for Living with Grace and Style* (2008) and *How To Be Lovely: The Audrey Hepburn Way of Life* (2005) draw on

Audrey Hepburn Syndrome: It's a Girl (and Sometimes a Boy) Thing
Jacqui Miller

Fig. 3: Dressed-down Holly croons 'Moon River'.

the spirit of Audrey, usually through extensive quotations, to advise on negotiating a path through 'happiness', 'success', health'. Other books, for example *So Audrey: 59 Ways to put a Little Hepburn in Your Step* (2011) imply it is only through drawing on Audrey as lifestyle guru that the fan may achieve her elegance. Along with the advice to wear 'sunglasses, the larger the better' and that 'you can never go wrong with a little black dress', another element of Audrey's persona, the 'saintly' UNICEF ambassador, is drawn on. A photograph of Audrey holding a child while smiling radiantly illustrates the tip to adopt 'compassion – it wears very well indeed'.

Audrey's class, elegance and style are so associated with the image of Holly Golightly, that sometimes a picture is all that is needed for Audrey's magic to take effect. *Things a Woman Should Know About Style* (2003) has a classic still from *Breakfast at Tiffany's* (see Figure 5) – Holly in evening dress gazing into the window the morning after the night before – but the book itself is a generic, not an 'Audrey' style guide.

Figure 4: Dressed down Carrie dances to 'Moon River'.

Perhaps surprisingly, it makes very few references to Audrey, just here and there in sections on ballet slippers and the little black dress. But it doesn't need to; the cover picture means that the fan will feel the Audrey magic on every page. Perhaps the self-help/style guide that most sums up Audrey's essential appeal, which is captured in its title, is Jordan Christy's *How To Be a Hepburn in a Hilton World: The Art of Living with Style, Class and Grace* (2009). Instructing young women to avoid the déclassé antics of current Z-listers, this book has the seal of approval of fans on *aparkavenueprincess. blogspot.com*. Awarding a 'Royal Rating' of a Holly-worthy four tiaras, the 'princess' deems that the book 'lives happily ever after on my bookshelf' because 'the resounding message that goes on throughout [...] is as timely, classy and unforgettable as Audrey herself'. The book even generated its own Facebook page for 'Hepburn Girls in a Hilton World' which achieved more than one thousand 'likes', including my own.

New Audreys/new fans
The electronic world has quite recently found a new way to bring Audrey to her fans. Online bookstore Amazon has literally dozens of Audrey-related items including biographies, calendars, photo albums and diaries. The innovation of the Kindle not only allows the 'regular' books to be bought in electronic form. Karina Hughes-Eperson's *How to Audrey: Hepburn Lessons in Love and Life* (2012) is the latest self-help/style guide but it is only available on the Kindle. Speaking to the 'traditions' of Audrey fandom in its attention to Audrey's 'fairy tales' and her status as a 'princess', it is also

Fig. 5: Even munching breakfast Holly/Audrey knows all
about style.

Fig. 6: Just Being Audrey
book trailer. Lessons little
girls may learn from Audrey's
example.

thoroughly rooted in the language of today's teenage fans
by its adoption of 'text-speak' terms such as 'thru'. Perhaps
the fact that the book advertises one of its assets as being
the ease with which it can be read in 15 minutes shows
that even Audrey's timelessness is not immune to Andy
Warhol's predictions about the time-limit of fame!

Print books also find new ways to extend Audrey's fandom. Margaret Cardillo (author) and Julia Denos (illustra-
tor) have produced in *Just Being Audrey* (2011) the kind
of book Audrey herself might have dreamed over as a girl.
The story is actually a factual account of the milestones
in Audrey's life, but rather than being written as a conventional biography, it casts Audrey as a character in her very
own fairy tale, and its originality is heightened because it
is not accompanied by photographs but by the kind of nostalgic illustrations seen in
a charming girl's storybook from the 1950s. Actually aimed at girls aged 4 to 8, this is
perhaps the first instance of a book deliberately fostering a new generation of Audrey
fans, something noted by Judy Baker, who posted an online review appreciating that it
brings Audrey's 'best qualities to life for a new generation of readers'. *Just Being Audrey* inspired book blogger the1stdaughter to initiate the process of 'Book Dreaming'
reserved for 'making you dreamy or possibly just end up making you dream about them'.
Asking 'Are you an Audrey Hepburn fan' she shares the book's charming animated trailer
in which its illustrations come to life.

As we can see, in this book, Audrey continues to be an example, presumably encour-
aging little girls to be disciplined, but the video's posting on YouTube generated chat
amongst the grown-up fandom. Ladyloveforevenmore admired the 1960s vibe of the
drawings, a time when Audrey Hepburn had a 'seminal influence on fashion', while an-
nalovesfilm focussed on Audrey as a star and a humanitarian: 'Wonderful actress with a
big heart […] Love Audrey'.

So far, Audrey's fandom has seemed to be exclusively female and strictly Euro-Amer-
ican, reflecting the lady herself. Of course, men fall in love with her; as a film studies
lecturer, as soon as men, from my next-door neighbour to taxi drivers to students dis-
cover my job, they wax lyrical about how Audrey Hepburn is their favourite actress. But
men and boys see her as an inspiration too, and as two recent novels show, Audrey is a
role model for global cultures. Rajeev Balasubramanyam is a British Asian author, whose
first novel creates Arjuna, a young girl living in a small South Indian town with her difficult family. In some ways, her life, full of struggles, but with a determination to escape
to better things, parallels Audrey's war-time experiences. To cope, she escapes into the
world of 1960s films, especially two of Audrey's, which also tell of girls born into hard
times who achieve transformation, *My Fair Lady* (George Cukor, 1964) and *Breakfast at*

Audrey Hepburn Syndrome: It's a Girl (and Sometimes a Boy) Thing
Jacqui Miller

Tiffany's. Seeing *Tiffany's* four times, by the third Arjuna almost believes that she *is* Holly, which carries her through difficult times. When her brother shouts at her as she walks upstairs, she pretends he is Mr Yunioshi, and when her family taunt her skinny frame, Arjuna takes comfort from her similarity to Audrey's slender build. Film-maker and author Alan Brown's novel, *Audrey Hepburn's Neck* (1996) again has Audrey as an inspiration, this time for Toshiyuki Okamota, a boy growing up above his father's noodle shop on Japan's most northerly island. On his ninth birthday he is taken to see *Roman Holiday* (William Wyler, 1953) by his mother, and while she is awestruck by the flawless line of Audrey's swan neck, his preference for western girls is formed from the moment she comes on-screen. The whole film is a tissue of references to Audrey and her films, every character seeming to love her and have a special Audrey moment, showing how truly transnational her fandom has become.

This transnationalism becomes even more apparent when surveying the extent of Audrey's online fansites. Just the first page of a Google search reveals French, Dutch and Italian sites, as well as, of course, UK and American, perhaps all countries with ties to her life and films. Less immediately obvious in associations are the Polish, German and Spanish sites, but the PokeCommunity also has an Audrey fan club, which in a way updates the nostalgia of *Audrey Hepburn's Neck* by fusing modern Japanese cartoonery with Audrey idolatry as Sango-the-demonslayer calls on other Audrey fans to join. There are probably literally countless Audrey fan clubs and sites as they are constantly being added to and extending their range. As well as the transnationality, they clearly cater to a range of focuses. *Audrey 1* is essentially a place for fans to meet and share information, *Adoring Audrey* principally celebrates her life and career, while *Simply Loverly* is a small site acting as a conduit to other links. Despite the vast numbers and nuanced appeals, all the Audrey sites are united in a common attitude, and again this sets them in contrast to the many, perhaps even more, sites that discuss Marilyn Monroe. Just as the majority of Monroe biographies focus one way or another on the 'tragedy' of her life, if not theories ranging from plausible to downright conspiratorial with regard to her death, the fansites also harp on her tragic passing and the need to pay homage to her memory, such as *Marilyn Remembered*, which is 'preserving the memory of Marilyn Monroe'. In contrast, for her fans, Audrey, or at least her spirit and influence, are very much alive. Monroe is to be pitied, Audrey is to be revered and her lead followed. It is impossible to find a site dedicated to her passing and unimaginable that fans would necessarily collectively mourn her death; they don't need to, her style is eternal and replicated every day. This is matched by the differing tone of the fandoms. On Marilyn's Facebook page a fan talks of getting a tattoo of her that takes up half their arm; it is impossible to imagine an Audrey fan expressing her fandom in this way. Instead, Audrey's fans always engage in what is almost a shared Audrey vocabulary. It is perhaps epitomized by the fansite *Rare Elegance*'s title, and the words Fan Pop member chose to describe Audrey. Thirty-three per cent polled 'elegant' while forty-seven voted 'classy' which takes us back to the results when typing 'Audrey' into the Boden catalogue.

Fans do not need to lament the loss of Audrey; her presence is everywhere. Audrey fan-fiction author, Capricornus 152, in a brief story about a young girl's influences identifies a new but welcome phenomenon. The girl, Taylor, reflects: 'she knew she had a terminal case of AHS (Audrey Hepburn Syndrome) and you know what? She liked it.' You know what? The fans have AHS. And they like it! ●

~~~~~~~~~~~~

GO FURTHER

Books

How to Audrey: Hepburn Lessons in Love and Life
Karina Hughes-Eperson
(Amazon Kindle, 2012)

So Audrey: 59 Ways to Put a Little Hepburn in Your Step
Cindy de la Hoz
(Philadelphia, PA: Running Press, 2011)

Just Being Audrey
Margaret Cardillo and Julia Denos
(New York: HarperCollins, 2011)

How To Be a Hepburn in a Hilton World: The Art of Living with Style, Class and Grace
Jordan Christie
(New York: Center Street, 2009)

What Would Audrey Do? Timeless Lessons for Living with Grace and Style
Pamela Clark Keogh
(London: Aurum, 2008)

Enchantment: The Life of Audrey Hepburn
Donald Spoto
(London: Hutchinson, 2006)

Audrey Hepburn: An Elegant Spirit
Sean Ferrer
(New York: Atria, 2005)

Audrey Hepburn Syndrome: It's a Girl (and Sometimes a Boy) Thing
Jacqui Miller

How To Be Lovely: The Audrey Hepburn Way of Life
Melissa Hellstern
(London: Robeson, 2005)

Things a Woman Should Know About Style
Karen Homer
(London: Prion, 2003)

In Beautiful Disguises
Rajeev Balasubramanyam
(London: Bloomsbury, 2000)

Audrey Style
Pamela Clarke Keogh and Hubert De Givenchy
(London: Aurum, 1999)

Sex and the City
Candace Bushnell
(New York: Warner Books, 1997)

Audrey Hepburn's Neck
Alan Brown
(Harpenden: Pocket Books 1996)

Audrey Hepburn: Fair Lady of the Screen
Ian Woodward
(London: Virgin Books, 1993)

Breakfast at Tiffany's
Truman Capote
(New York: Randon House, 1958)

The House of Mirth
Edith Wharton
(New York: Scribner, 1905)

Film/Television

'A "Vogue" Idea', Martha Coolidge, dir. *Sex and the City* (New York: NY: HBO, 2002).
'I Heart New York', Martha Coolidge, dir. *Sex and the City* (New York: HBO, 2002).

'No Ifs, Ands, or Butts' Nicole Holofcener, dir., *Sex and the City* (New York, NY: HBO, 2000).
'Sex and the City', Susan Seidelman, dir., *Sex and the City* (New York, NY: HBO, 1998).
The Age of Innocence, Martin Scorsese, dir. (USA: Columbia Pictures, 1993).
An Affair to Remember, Leo McCarey, dir. (USA: Twentieth Century Fox, 1957).

Online

Park Avenue Princess [Blogspot], aparkavenueprincessblogspot.com

Hepburn Girls in a Hilton World [Facebook group], *The 1ˢᵗ Daughter*, the1stdaughter.blogspot.co.uk

'Just Being Audrey video' [YouTube], 13 January 2011, .
'Just being Audrey'
Judy Baker
Amazon.com
February 6, 2011
http://www.amazon.com/review/R1465WUXBMQQ5/ref=cm_cr_pr_viewpnt#R-1465WUXBMQQ5

The PokeCommunity
Audrey 1, Adoring Audrey [Tumblr], *Simply Loverly* [Freewebs], *Marilyn Remembered* [Blogspot], Marilyn Monroe [Facebook page], *Rare Elegance*, 'The Audrey Hepburn Syndrome'
Capricornus152 (pseud.)
FanFiction.Net. 12 April 2010, http://www.fanfiction.net/s/5892391/1/The-Audrey-Hepburn-Syndrome.

Contributor Details

EDITOR

Dr. Jacqui Miller is Senior Lecturer in Visual Communication and Subject Leader for Media and Communication programmes at Liverpool Hope University. She is deputy series editor for Liverpool Hope's multi-volume series on Ethics and has edited a volume on Ethics and Film Studies, contributing a chapter on Warner Bros. and the making of *Confessions of a Nazi Spy*. Particularly interested in the relationship between film, culture and history, Dr. Miller has published on a range of subjects from the meaning of Europe in the Riplead novels and Films, to post-World War II American cultural colonisation in New German Cinema. She leads Liverpool Hope's popular Culture Research Group and hosts the annual international conference, Theorising the Popular at Hope each July.

CONTRIBUTORS

Dr. Lynn Hilditch is an independent researcher in art history and photography based at Liverpool Hope University. Lynn has lectured on various aspects of the visual arts (predominantly American film and photography); her research interests include the interpretation of war in art and photography and the socio-historical representation of gender in twentieth-century popular culture.

Andrew Howe is an Associate Professor in the Department of History at La Sierra University where he teaches courses in American history, popular culture, and film studies. Although a generalist by nature, with recent projects involving such widely disparate research subjects as the history of the hot dog and the FIFA World Cup as a means of negotiating political conflict, particular areas of interest include the Science Fiction genre, the films of Alfred Hitchcock, and World War II. He is currently working on a book length project focusing upon how biological invasions, extinctions, and re-introductions are covered by the media. To that end, a recent sabbatical explored the manner in which the Africanized (Killer) Bee "invasion" of the late 1970s/early 1980s was constructed as a threat by employing metaphors and terminologies culled from that era's debates about illegal immigration.

Armen Karaoghlanian is a graduate of the USC School of Cinematic Arts. In his career, he has continuously maintained a balance between film studies and film production, observing cinema through the lens of a film scholar and filmmaker. Armen is a contributing writer for *Yerevan Magazine*, writing both in print and online with his cinema column, *From the Vault*, dedicated to the discussion of Armenian cinema. Armen is also the co-creator and writer of *Interiors*, an online film and architecture journal, in which films are examined in terms of space. In addition, his films have screened in film festivals nationwide, while his writing has been featured in a number of publications, including *MUBI*, *ArchDaily*, *Daily Mail*, *la Repubblica*, *Volume Magazine* and *Azure Magazine*. In July 2012, he was welcomed onto the set of Atom Egoyan's *Devil's Knot* in Atlanta, Georgia and recorded a daily diary of the production of the film. Armen is currently offering a course in media at Woodbury University.

Peter Krämer is a Senior Lecturer in Film Studies at the University of East Anglia (Norwich, UK). He is the author of A Clockwork Orange (Palgrave, 2011), 2001: A Space Odyssey (BFI, 2010) and The New Hollywood: From Bonnie and Clyde to Star Wars (Wallflower Press, 2005), and the co-editor of Screen Acting (Routledge, 1999) and The Silent Cinema Reader (Routledge, 2004). He also co-wrote a book for children entitled American Film: An A-Z Guide (Franklin Watts, 2003).

Dr. Esperanza Miyake currently teaches Media Studies and Cultural Studies at Liverpool John Moores University, including the Mass Communications summer programme. Her PhD thesis was on Queer Ethnographies of Music and Sexuality. She has and continues to present, publish and review works on popular culture, music, and race/raciality, particularly in relation to sexuality. She is the author of the award-winning essay, 'My, is that Cyborg a Little Queer?' (*IJWS*, 2004). She is the co-editor (with Dr Adi Kuntsman) of *Out of Place: Interrogating Silences in Queerness/Raciality* (Raw Nerve, 2008).

Dr. Claire Molloy is Professor of Film, Television and Digital Media at Edge Hill University. Her publications include the books *Memento* (2010), *Popular Media and Animals* (2011), *Beyond Human: from animality to transhumanism* (2012) and *American Independent Cinema: indie, indiewood and beyond* (2012). She has published widely on media industries, American cinema, film and politics, digital activism, environment, nature and animal ethics.

Francis Vose is a Professional Tutor at Liverpool Hope University teaching filmmaking, animation and photography to undergraduate and post-graduate students. Before taking up an academic post, Francis was the Creative Director at Cosgrove Hall Films, where he was responsible for the making of numerous animated TV series. Francis has won many awards for his work including an International Emmy for best animated film – The Fool of the World and the Flying Ship, 3 BAFTAs for best animated series – The Wind in the Willows, British Animation Awards for best TV series – Bill and Ben – Cbeebies, RTS Award for best animated series – Little Robots – Cbeebies and Chicago International Film Festival for best animated film – The Fool of the World and the Flying Ship.

Audrey Hepburn Filmography

Nederlands in Zeven Lessen/Dutch in Seven Lessons or *Dutch at the Double*, Charles Huguenot Van der Linden, dir. (Netherlands: G-B Instructional Production, 1948)
One Wild Oat, Charles Saunders, dir. (UK: Eros-Coronet, 1951)
Young Wives' Tale, Henry Cass, dir. (UK: Associated British Pictures, 1951)
Laughter in Paradise, Mario Zampi, dir. (UK: Associated British Pictures, 1951)
The Lavender Hill Mob, Charles Crichton, dir. (UK: Ealing Studios, 1951)
The Secret People, Sidney Cole, dir. (UK: Ealing Studios, 1952)
Nous Irons a Monte Carlo/Monte Carlo Baby, Jean Boyer and Lester Fuller, dir. (France: GFD/Favorite Pictures, 1952)
Roman Holiday, William Wyler, dir. (USA: Paramount, 1953)
Sabrina, dir. Billy Wilder (USA: Paramount, 1954)
War and Peace, King Vidor, dir. (Italy/USA: Ponti-De Laurentis Productions/Paramount, 1956)
Funny Face, Stanley Donen, dir. (USA: Paramount, 1957)
Love in the Afternoon, Billy Wilder, dir. (USA: Allied Artists, 1957)
The Nun's Story, Fred Zinnemann, dir. (USA: Warner Brothers, 1959)
Green Mansions, Mel Ferrer, dir. (USA: Metro-Goldwyn-Meyer, 1959)
The Unforgiven, John Huston, dir. (USA: Hecht-Hill-Lancaster Productions, 1960)
Breakfast at Tiffany's, Blake Edwards, dir. (USA: Paramount, 1961)
The Children's Hour, William Wyler, dir. (USA: United Artists, 1961)
Charade, Stanley Donen, dir. (USA: Universal, 1963)
Paris When it Sizzles, Richard Quine, dir. (USA: Paramount, 1964)
My Fair Lady, George Cukor, dir. (USA: Warner Brothers, 1964)
How to Steal a Million, William Wyler, dir. (USA: Twentieth Century Fox, 1966)
Two for the Road, Stanley Donen, dir. (USA: Twentieth Century Fox, 1967)
Wait Until Dark, Terence Young, dir. (USA: Warner Brothers, 1967)
Robin and Marion, Richard Lester, dir. (UK: Columbia, 1976)
Bloodline, Terence Young, dir. (USA: Paramount, 1979)
They All Laughed, Peter Bogdanovich, dir. (USA: Time-Life Films/Twentieth Century Fox, 1981)
Always, Steven Spielberg, dir. (USA: Universal-United Artists, 1990)

'A GIRL CAN'T READ THAT SORT OF THING WITHOUT HER LIPSTICK'.

HOLLY GOLIGHTLY IN
BREAKFAST AT TIFFANY'S

Image Credits

From *Roman Holiday* (the film)
Chapter 1: Figs. 1-2 pages 10-11, Chapter 2: Fig. 3 page 23,
Chapter 7: Figs. 4-6 pages 72-73, Chapter 8: Fig. 1 page 77
From *Sabrina* (the film)
Chapter 1: Figs. 3-4 pages 12-13, Chapter 2: Figs. 3-4 page 23,
Chapter 4: Fig. 3 page 39, Chapter 7: Fig. 7 page 74, Chapter 8: Figs. 2-4 pages 78-79
From *Breakfast at Tiffany's* (the film)
Chapter 1: Figs. 5-6 page 14, Chapter 2: Fig. 7 page 26, Chapter 5: Fig. 7 page 53,
Chapter 8: Fig. 7 page 82, Chapter 10: Fig. 3 page 100, Chapter 10: Fig. 5 page 101
From *Funny Face* (the film)
Chapter 1: Fig. 7-8 pages 15-16, Chapter 2: Fig. 6 page 25,
Chapter 4: Fig. 2 page 39, Chapter 8: Figs. 5-6 pages 80-81
From *My Fair Lady* (the film)
Chapter 1: Figs. 9-10 pages 16-17, Chapter 3: Figs. 1-13 pages 31-37
From *Laughter in Paradise* (the film)
Chapter 2: Fig. 2 page 22, Chapter 7: Fig. 1 page 71
From *The Secret People* (the film)
Chapter 6: Figs. 1-2 page 60, Chapter 7: Fig. 3 page 72
From *War and Peace* (the film)
Chapter 6: Figs. 3-4 pages 61-62
From *The Unforgiven* (the film)
Chapter 6: Fig. 5 page 63
From *Green Mansions* (the film)
Chapter 6: Fig. 6 page 64
From *Two for the Road* (the film)
Chapter 6: Figs. 7-8 page 65, Chapter 8: Fig. 8 page 83
From *The Lavender Hill Mob* (the film)
Chapter 7 Fig. 2 page 71

Additional Images
Chapter 2:   Fig. 1 page 21 Courtesy of Jacqui Miller
Chapter 4:   Fig. 1 page 39 from Will and Grace 'The Buying Game', Season 1, episode 8
    Fig. 4 page 40 http://www.lenasottomayor.com
    Fig. 5 page 40 http://www.youtube.com
    Fig. 6 page 44 http://www.youtube.com
Chapter 5:   Fig. 1 page 49 http://osatelegraph.org/the-origins-of-the-little-black-dress/
    Fig. 2 page 50 http://cocolovecity.wordpress.com/
    Fig. 3 page 51 http://rufiojones.wordpress.com/2011/03/17/cartoon-black-history-betty-boop/
    Fig. 4 page 51 http://en.wikipedia.org/wiki/Rosie_the_Riveter
    Fig. 5 page 52 http://4yournformation.wordpress.com/category/fashion/

FAN PHENOMENA

OTHER TITLES AVAILABLE IN THE SERIES

Star Trek
Edited by Bruce E. Drushel
ISBN: 978-1-78320-023-8
£15.50 / $22

Star Wars
Edited by Mika Elovaara
ISBN: 978-1-78320-022-1
£15.50 / $22

The Big Lebowski
Edited by Zachary Ingle
ISBN: 978-1-78320-202-7
£15.50 / $22

The Big Lebowski
Edited by Lynn Zubernis
and Katherine Larsen
ISBN: 978-1-78320-203-4
£15.50 / $22

Doctor Who
Edited by Paul Booth
ISBN: 978-1-78320-020-7
£15.50 / $22

Buffy the Vampire Slayer
Edited by Jennifer K. Stuller
ISBN: 978-1-78320-019-1
£15.50 / $22

Twin Peaks
Edited by Marisa C. Hayes
and Franck Boulegue
ISBN: 978-1-78320-024-5
£15.50 / $22

Audrey Hepburn
Edited by Jacqui Miller
ISBN: 978-1-78320-206-5
£15.50 / $22

For further information about the series
and news of forthcoming titles visit **www.intellectbooks.com**